# 英语的逻辑
## 30天学会美国人的英语逻辑

The Logic of English!

刘婉瑀◎著

北京理工大学出版社
BEIJING INSTITUTE OF TECHNOLOGY PRESS

# User's Guide 使用说明

## 🗨 Step1 学习美国人的发音方式

### ❶ 美国人都是这样发音

美国人不用学 KK 音标，自然而然建立起独特的发音规则。Part 1 为读者归纳整理出美国人的发音规则，以及课本上学不到的不规则发音方式。

### ❷ 边听边说才能学会

要真正学会美国人发音的腔调与节奏起伏，一定要多加练习，除了听 MP3 之外，更要跟着开口说，反复几次直到熟练，才能达成有效学习。

★ 本书附赠音频为 MP3 格式 ★

# ●Step2 学习美国人的常用单词

### ❸ 美国人都说这几个单词

美国人每天最常使用的单词其实不到1 000个。Part 2为读者挑选出日常生活中使用频率最高的单词,例如表达"增加"的单词add、表示"变成"的单词become,再加以延伸。

### ❹ 依单词群组分类学习

根据各单元主要单词,延伸学习相关的"单词群",例如与add相关的单词群,就包括表达"数量变多""数量变少",以及表示"计算"的各个单词。

### ❺ 按单词大小分别记忆

每一群组的相关单词,都依其在日常生活中的使用频率标示重要性,分为"✿✿✿三颗星""✿✿两颗星"及"✿一颗星"三种等级,单词也按照"大""中""小"来区分。级别越大的单词表示使用频率越高,可以先从这几个单词开始学习。

### ❻ 阅读例句,加深印象

每个单词都附上实用例句,让读者明白单词的正确用法。仔细阅读例句,可加深对单词的印象,并且学会活用。

〔词性符号说明〕
- ⓝ 名词
- ⓥ 动词
- ⓐ 形容词

# User's Guide 使用说明

## Step 3 学习美国人的日常会话

### ⑦ 美国人都说这几句会话

美国人聊天时,说来说去不外乎那几个句型和惯用语。Part 3 将介绍生活中的常用惯用语,例如:要询问"发生什么事"就说"What happened",要表达"觉得不舒服"可以说"under the weather"。

### ⑧ 依相关情境分类学习

根据各单元主要情境,延伸学习相关的"会话群",例如与"认同"相关的会话,就包括表达"同意与附议"、"反对与不相信",以及表示"不知道、不理解"的实用句型。

### ⑨ 从简单的句子开始学

每一群组的相关句型,都依其使用频率及难易度来标示,分为"大星"、"中星"及"小星"三种等级,句子也按照"大""中""小"来区别。级别越大的句子表示使用频率越高,可以先从这几个句子开始学习。

### ⑩ 美国人聊天实例学习

收录美国人聊天时的实际对话范例,让读者更熟悉前面学习到的句型。另外,每一课都补充相关的惯用语,帮助读者说出最地道的美式英语。

004

The Logic of English!

## Part1 跟美国人学自然发音

**Lesson 01** | 美式英语的发音规则1　002

**Lesson 02** | 美式英语的发音规则2　007

**Lesson 03** | 学习美国人的腔调与节奏　023

## Part2 美国人最常用的单词

**Lesson 04** | 东西总是越加越多→ add　032

**Lesson 05** | 我有好消息要宣布→ announce　040

**Lesson 06** | 事情总是变来变去→ become　047

**Lesson 07** | 多多赞美与鼓励吧→ best　055

**Lesson 08** | 都关心些什么事呢→ concern　062

**Lesson 09** | 做决定真的不容易→ decide　069

**Lesson 10** │ 行为与举止要得体→ **decent**　076

**Lesson 11** │ 跟随我，你会了解我→ **follow**　083

**Lesson 12** │ 事情一定有所改善→ **improve**　091

**Lesson 13** │ 有好多事情要学习→ **learn**　098

**Lesson 14** │ 外表看起来怎么样→ **look**　105

**Lesson 15** │ 我的心里非常介意→ **mind**　112

**Lesson 16** │ 问题好多，困难重重→ **problem**　119

**Lesson 17** │ 了解事情的严重性→ **serious**　125

**Lesson 18** │ 了解用途，善加利用→ **use**　133

## Part 3　美国人聊天都说这些话

**Lesson 19** │ 你惹毛我了→
　　　　　　**You're Getting on My Nerves**　142

**Lesson 20** │ 人各有喜好→
　　　　　　**There Is No Accounting for Tastes**　149

**Lesson 21** │ 身体不舒服→ **Under the Weather**　159

**Lesson 22** │ 无聊透顶→ **It Bores Me to Death**　168

**Lesson 23** | 冷静下来→ Calm Down　177

**Lesson 24** | 易如反掌→ As Easy As Pie　186

**Lesson 25** | 很聪明的人→ A Smart Cookie　195

**Lesson 26** | 祝你好运→ Break a Leg　204

**Lesson 27** | 事情悬而未决→ Up in the Air　213

**Lesson 28** | 非常出色→ With Flying Colors　222

**Lesson 29** | 难得一见→ Once in a Blue Moon　230

**Lesson 30** | 我也这么觉得→ Great Minds Think Alike　239

Step1　建构基础发音
Step2　单词群组记忆
Step3　常用英语会话

30天学会美国人的英语逻辑！

跟美国人学自然发音

Part 1

# Lesson 01
# 美式英语的发音规则 1

本章我们要学习的是自然拼读法（Phonics）。自然拼读法顾名思义就是看到英语单词能够自然念出来，听到单词发音也能够自然把单词拼出来。

本单元帮助读者轻松、快速、有效率地学习自然拼读的规则，并且没有太过复杂的术语。当我们熟悉了自然拼读的基本规则之后，就能掌握大部分的英语单词。此外，本单元也将介绍 KK 音标，学习自然拼读的辅助工具。自然拼读加上 KK 音标，让英语学习事半功倍！

建议读者可先熟悉英语单词，再去对照发音规则。规则供参考用，千万不要死记硬背，这样才不会一开始就在规则中晕头转向！一定要多念、多听、多看、多练习，毕竟语言不是死板的公式，而是要活用的沟通工具！另外，本书帮读者整理出的基本发音规则，可运用于大部分单词。但是"凡规则必有例外"，只有多阅读、多学习，才能掌握规则之外的发音。

在认识自然拼读之前，先了解发音的基本组成：

- 我们平常所念的 26 个字母（A、B、C、D、E、F、G……）是字母的"名称"。
- 在自然拼读里，看字发音时所使用的则是字母的"发音"。

## 英语 26 个字母大小写与字母发音

| Aa [ei] | Bb [bi] | Cc [si] | Dd [di] | Ee [i] | Ff [ef] |
|---|---|---|---|---|---|
| Gg [dʒi] | Hh [eitʃ] | Ii [ai] | Jj [dʒei] | Kk [kei] | Ll [el] |
| Mm [em] | Nn [en] | Oo [əu] | Pp [pi] | Qq [kju] | Rr [a:(r)] |
| Ss [es] | Tt [ti] | Uu [ju] | Vv [vi] | Ww [ˈdʌblju] | Xx [eks] |
| Yy [wai] | Zz [zi] | | | | |

**提醒**
- 自然拼读法中字母按发音分成元音与辅音。

## 字母 A-Z 字母发音分类

| 元音 | a, e, i, o, u |
|---|---|
| 辅音 | b, c, d, f, g, h, j, k, l, m, n, p, q, r, s, t, v, w, x, y, z |

## KK 音标基本分类

| 元音 | 单元音 | [i] [ɪ] [e] [ɛ] [æ] [ɑ] [o] [ɔ] [u] [ʊ] [ə] [ʌ] [ɚ] [ɜ] |
|---|---|---|
| | 双元音 | [aɪ] [au] [ɔɪ] |

| 辅音 | 浊辅音 | [b] [d] [g] [v] [z] [ð] [ʒ] [dʒ] [l] [r] [m] [n] [ŋ] [j] [w] |
|---|---|---|
| | 清辅音 | [h] [f] [k] [p] [s] [t] [tʃ] [ʃ] [θ] |

## 自然发音基本规则整理

### 元音篇 ----- 发音 ------- 字母组合

**短元音**

| 发音 | 字母组合 |
|---|---|
| [æ] | a |
| [ɛ] | e / ea |
| [ɪ] | i / y |
| [ɚ] | e / v |
| [ə] | o / u |

**长元音**

| 发音 | 字母组合 |
|---|---|
| [ɑ] | o |
| [ʌ] | u / o / oo / ou |
| [ʊ] | u / oo |
| [ɔ] | al / au / aw |
| [e] | a_e / ai / ay / eigh |
| [i] | ea / e_e / ee / ei / ie / ey |
| [aɪ] | i_e / ie / igh / y |
| [o] | oa / oe / o_e / ow |
| [u] | ew / ue / u_e / ui / oo |

★ 元音在轻音节时，发 [ə] 的音。

### 辅音篇 ----- 发音 ------- 字母组合

**浊辅音**

| 发音 | 字母组合 |
|---|---|
| [b] | b / bb |
| [d] | d / dd |
| [g] | g / gg / gh / gu |

| 辅音篇 | 发音 | 字母组合 |
|---|---|---|
| 浊辅音 | [dʒ] | j / ge / gi / gy / dge |
| | [ʒ] | si / su |
| | [v] | v / ve / f |
| | [l] | l / ll |
| | [m] | m / mm |
| | [n] | n / nn |
| | [ŋ] | ng / nk |
| | [r] | r / rr / wr / rh |
| | [w] | w / wh / o |
| | [j] | y |
| | [z] | z / zz / s / se / ss |
| | [h] | h |
| 清辅音 | [p] | p / pp |
| | [t] | t / tt / ed |
| | [k] | c / k / ck / ch / que |
| | [f] | f / ff |
| | [s] | s / ss / se / sc / ce / ci / cy |

| 辅音篇 | 发音 | 字母组合 |
|---|---|---|
| 清辅音 | [tʃ] | ch / tch / tu |
| | [ʃ] | sh / ti / c / s / ss / ch |
| | [θ] | th |

## 自然发音的特殊组合

| 规则 | 发音 | 字母组合 |
|---|---|---|
| 元音 + r | [ɑr] | ar |
| | [ɜ] | er / ir / or / ur |
| | [ɚ] | ar / er / or |
| | [ɔr] | ar / or |
| 其他元音 + r | [ɛr] | air / are / ear / ere |
| | [ɪr] | ear / ere / eer |
| | [or] | oor / ore / our |
| 特殊元音组合 | [aʊ] | ou / ow |
| | [ɔɪ] | oi / oy |

★ 在某些单词中不发音的辅音：**b, h, l, t, w, g, gh, k, p, s**

# 美式英语的发音规则 2

## 元音篇

提醒
- 先熟悉单词,再去对应规则!

### 短元音

| a [æ] | 字母组合 | 例　词 |
|---|---|---|
| | 字母发音 | act 行动 / add 增加 / amp. 电吉他 / ant 蚂蚁 / ax 斧 |
| | 在两个辅音中间 | bad 坏的 / cat 猫 / hat 帽子 / lab 实验室 / pat 轻拍 |

| e [ɛ] | 字母组合 | 例　词 |
|---|---|---|
| | 字母发音 | ebb 退潮 / Edward 艾德华 / empty 空的 / end 结束 / epic 史诗 |
| | 在两个辅音中间 | best 最好的 / def 一流的 / jet 喷射机 / send 寄 / wet 湿的 |
| | ea | bread 面包 / dead 死的 / head 头 / health 健康 / tear 撕 |

| | 字母组合 | 例 词 |
|---|---|---|
| **i**<br>[I] | 字母发音 | idiom 成语 / ignite 点燃 / ill 生病的 / image 图像 / ink 墨水 |
| | 在两个辅音中间 | big 大的 / fish 鱼 / give 给 / milk 牛奶 / wind 风 |
| | **y** | gym 体育馆 / happy 快乐的 / myth 神话 / washy 水分多的 |

| | 字母组合 | 例 词 |
|---|---|---|
| **o**<br>[ɑ] | 字母发音 | odd 奇特的 / omelet 煎蛋卷 / on 在……上 / opt 选择 / otto 玫瑰油 |
| | 在两个辅音中间 | clock 时钟 / mob 暴民 / rob 抢劫 / sock 短袜 / stop 停止 |

| | 字母组合 | 例 词 |
|---|---|---|
| **u**<br>[ʌ] | 字母发音 | ugly 丑的 / unsafe 不安全的 / up 在上面 / us 我们 / utter 说 |
| | 在两个辅音中间 | cut 切 / fun 乐趣 / hug 拥抱 / mud 泥巴 / run 跑 |
| | **o** | come 来 / dove 鸽子 / honey 蜂蜜 / mother 母亲 / onion 洋葱 |
| | **oo** | blood 血 / flood 洪水 |
| | **ou** | double 两倍的 / touch 抚摸 / trouble 麻烦 / young 年轻的 |

| | 字母组合 | 例 词 |
|---|---|---|
| [ʊ] | **u** | bull 公牛 / full 满的 / pudding 布丁 / push 推 / put 放 |
| | **oo** | book 书 / good 好的 / hood 连在外套上的帽子 / look 看 / wood 木头 |

| | 字母组合 | 例　　词 |
|---|---|---|
| [ɔ] | al | all 全部的 / bald 秃头 / chalk 粉笔 / talk 谈话 / walk 走路 |
| | au | August 八月 / cause 原因 / fraud 欺诈 / launch 发射 / pause 暂停 |
| | aw | dawn 黎明 / hawk 老鹰 / law 法律 |

## 长元音

| | 字母组合 | 例　　词 |
|---|---|---|
| [e] | a_e | ate 吃 / bake 烘焙 / cake 蛋糕 / hate 恨 / late 迟的 |
| | ai | aid 援助 / maid 少女 / nail 钉子 / paint 油漆 / sail 航行 |
| | ay | bay 湾 / day 一天 / hay 干草 / may 可能 / stay 停留 |
| | eigh | eight 八 / neigh 马嘶 / weight 重量 |

| | 字母组合 | 例　　词 |
|---|---|---|
| [i] | ea | cream 奶油 / leap 跳跃 / meat 肉 / read 阅读 / tea 茶 |
| | e_e | cede 割让 / compete 竞争 / complete 完整的 / gene 基因 / these 这些 |
| | ee | cheek 脸颊 / freeze 结冰 / peek 偷看 / seek 寻找 / weep 哭泣 |
| | ei | ceiling 天花板 / conceit 自大 / deceit 欺骗 / receipt 收据 / receive 收到 |
| | ie | diesel 柴油 / field 领域 / grief 悲伤 / pier 码头 / shield 盾牌 |
| | ey | key 钥匙 |

| | 字母组合 | 例 词 |
|---|---|---|
| [aɪ] | i_e | bike 单车 / dice 骰子 / like 喜欢 / time 时间 |
| | ie | die 死亡 / lie 说谎 / pie 派 / tie 绑 |
| | igh | fight 打架 / high 高的 / night 夜晚 / right 对的 |
| | y | cry 哭泣 / fly 飞 / sky 天空 / try 尝试 |

| | 字母组合 | 例 词 |
|---|---|---|
| [o] | oa | coal 煤 / goat 山羊 / oak 橡树 / roast 烤 |
| | oe | doe 雌鹿 / foe 敌人 / Joe 乔 / toe 脚趾 |
| | o_e | bone 骨头 / hope 希望 / pole 杆 / rope 绳索 |
| | ow | arrow 箭 / elbow 手肘 / pillow 枕头 |

| | 字母组合 | 例 词 |
|---|---|---|
| [ju] | ew | dew 露水 / few 几乎没有；少数（否定）/ new 新的 |
| | u_e | excuse 借口 / nude 裸体的 / use 使用 |
| | ue | barbecue 烤肉 / cue 暗示 / issue 问题 |

| | 字母组合 | 例 词 |
|---|---|---|
| [u] | ew | chew 咀嚼 / crew 工作人员 / grew 成长 |
| | ue | blue 蓝色的 / glue 胶水 / true 真实的 |
| | u_e | flute 长笛 / rude 粗鲁的 / rule 规则 |
| | ui | bruise 瘀青 / fruit 水果 / juice 果汁 |
| | oo | food 食物 / mood 心情 / room 房间 |

## 补充：元音在轻音节时，发 [ə] 的音。

| | 字母组合 | 例　词 |
|---|---|---|
| [ə] | a | advance 促进 / again 再次 / ago 以前 |
| | e | maven 专家 / open 打开 |
| | o | provide 提供 / season 季节 / together 一起 |
| | u | circus 马戏团 / crocus 藏红花 |

### 辅音篇

- 本单元学习辅音的发音规则。
- 辅音分成浊辅音以及清辅音。
- 较特别的部分还包括双辅音。

## 浊辅音

| | 字母组合 | 例　词 |
|---|---|---|
| [b] | b | ban 禁令 / bar 酒吧 / benefit 利益 |
| | bb | cabbage 甘蓝菜 / rabbit 兔子 |

| | 字母组合 | 例　词 |
|---|---|---|
| [d] | d | dark 黑暗的 / desire 渴望 / discuss 讨论 |
| | dd | middle 中间的 / wedding 婚礼 |

| | 字母组合 | 例　　词 |
|---|---|---|
| [g] | g | bag 袋子 / frog 青蛙 / gap 差距 / gold 黄金 |
| | gg | doggy 小狗 / giggle 傻笑 / legging 打底裤 |
| | gh | Ghana 加纳 / ghastly 可怕的 / ghost 鬼 |
| | gu | guess 猜 / guest 宾客 / guide 指导 |

| | 字母组合 | 例　　词 |
|---|---|---|
| [dʒ] | j | jigsaw 拼图玩具 / jinx 厄运 |
| | ge | age 年纪 / forge 锻造 / strange 陌生的 |
| | gi | apologize 道歉 / giant 巨大的 / magic 魔术 |
| | gy | apology 道歉 / biology 生物学 / stingy 小气的 |
| | dge | badge 徽章 / judge 判决 / ridge 山脊 |

| | 字母组合 | 例　　词 |
|---|---|---|
| [ʒ] | si | conclusion 结论 / television 电视 |
| | su | exposure 爆炸 / leisure 悠闲 / treasure 珍藏 |

| | 字母组合 | 例　　词 |
|---|---|---|
| [v] | v | valid 有效的 / view 视野 / vital 致命的 |
| | ve | curve 曲线 / live 活着 / wave 波浪 |
| | f | of ……的 |

| | 字母组合 | 例 词 |
|---|---|---|
| [l] | l | last 持续 / lead 领导 / lion 狮子 / liter 公升 |
| | ll | bell 钟 / ell 侧房 / hell 地狱 / tell 告诉 |

| | 字母组合 | 例 词 |
|---|---|---|
| [m] | m | aim 目标 / man 男人 / woman 女人 |
| | mm | comma 逗号 / hammer 榔头 / mommy 妈妈 |

| | 字母组合 | 例 词 |
|---|---|---|
| [n] | n | crayon 蜡笔 / nature 自然 / nerve 神经 |
| | nn | Anna 安娜 / annex 附加 / dinner 晚餐 |

| | 字母组合 | 例 词 |
|---|---|---|
| [ŋ] | ng | according 相符的 / wrong 错的 |
| | nk（k有发音） | bank 银行 / drink 喝 / stink 糟透的 |

| | 字母组合 | 例 词 |
|---|---|---|
| [r] | r | near 附近的 / rat 老鼠 / risk 风险 |
| | rr | arrange 安排 / array 整队 / cherry 樱桃 |
| | wr（w不发音） | wreck 船难 / wrestle 摔跤 / wrinkle 皱纹 / wrist 腕关节 / write 写 |
| | rh（h不发音） | rhapsody 狂想曲 / rhino 犀牛 / rhomb 菱形 / rhyme 韵脚 / rhythm 节奏 |

| [w] | 字母组合 | 例　词 |
|---|---|---|
| | w | warm 温暖的 / weather 天气 / worth 价值 |
| | wh（h不发音） | what 什么 / when 何时 / whereas 反之 / which 哪一个 / while 一会儿 |
| | o | once 一次 / one 一个 |

| [j] | 字母组合 | 例　词 |
|---|---|---|
| | y | yawn 呵欠 / yet 还没 / yield 产生 / you 你 |

| [z] | 字母组合 | 例　词 |
|---|---|---|
| | z | zero 零 / zombie 僵尸 / zoo 动物园 |
| | zz | blizzard 暴风雪 / jazz 爵士乐 / puzzle 谜 |
| | s | desert 沙漠 / music 音乐 / raisin 葡萄干 |
| | se | cheese 奶酪 / nose 鼻子 / please 请 |
| | ss | dessert 甜点 / dissolve 分解 / scissors 剪刀 |

## 清辅音

| [h] | 字母组合 | 例　词 |
|---|---|---|
| | h | Halloween 万圣节 / hand 手 / hide 隐藏 |

| [p] | 字母组合 | 例　词 |
|---|---|---|
| | p | pet 宠物 / police 警察 / whisper 低语 |
| | pp | happy 快乐的 / hippo 河马 / pepper 胡椒 |

| | 字母组合 | 例　词 |
|---|---|---|
| [t] | t | technology 科技 / tired 疲倦的 / tour 旅行 |
| | tt | attach 系上 / attain 获得 / butter 奶油 |
| | Ved<br>（过去式）<br>无声字尾 +<br>ed / d | asked 问 / hoped 希望 / kissed 吻 / laughed 笑 / washed 洗 |

| | 字母组合 | 例　词 |
|---|---|---|
| [k] | c | car 汽车 / cocoon 茧 / consider 考虑 |
| | k | kangaroo 袋鼠 / kick 踢 / king 国王 |
| | ck | attack 攻击 / buck 雄鹿 / dock 码头 / lock 锁 |
| | ch | ache 痛 / chemistry 化学 / orchid 兰花 |
| | que | antique 古董 / boutique 时装店 |

| | 字母组合 | 例　词 |
|---|---|---|
| [f] | f | fall 跌倒 / feature 特征 / film 电影 |
| | ff | affection 感情 / coffee 咖啡 / offend 冒犯 |

| | 字母组合 | 例　词 |
|---|---|---|
| [s] | s | salt 盐 / sign 记号 / soul 灵魂 / subject 主题 |
| | ss | bless 为……祝福 / dress 打扮 / floss 牙线 |
| | se | house 房子 / mouse 老鼠 / promise 承诺 |
| | sc | ascend 上升 / scene 现场 / science 科学 |

| [s] | ce | concept 概念 / embrace 拥抱 / voice 声音 |
|---|---|---|
| | ci | accident 事故 / civil 公民的 / exercise 运动 |
| | cy | agency 机构 / mercy 怜悯 / vacancy 空白 |

★ c 在 e、i、y 前发 [s]。

## 双辅音

| | 字母组合 | 例　　词 |
|---|---|---|
| [tʃ] | ch | approach 走近 / cheat 欺骗 / chic 时髦的 |
| | tch | catch 接住 / ditch 壕沟 / kitchen 厨房 |
| | tu | mixture 混合 / posture 姿势 / torture 折磨 |

| | 字母组合 | 例　　词 |
|---|---|---|
| [ʃ] | sh | anguish 苦恼 / blush 脸红 / shudder 发抖 |
| | ti | education 教育 / location 地点 / tradition 传统 |
| | c | ocean 海洋 / official 官方的 / special 特别的 |
| | s | Asia 亚洲 / insurance 保险 / sugar 糖 |
| | ss | assure 担保 / confession 坦承 |
| | ch | brochure 手册 / champagne 香槟 |

| | 字母组合 | 例　　词 |
|---|---|---|
| [θ] | th | theory 理论 / think 思考 / thunder 雷声 |

| [f] | 字母组合 | 例词 |
|---|---|---|
| | ph | photo 照片 / phrase 短语 / physics 物理学 |
| | gh | cough 咳嗽 / enough 足够的 / laugh 笑 |

### 自然发音的特殊组合

- 本单元学习自然发音规则以外的常见特殊组合。
- 包括元音组合、元音加 r 的组合、不发音的辅音、混合辅音。

## 特殊元音组合

| [au] | 字母组合 | 例词 |
|---|---|---|
| | ou | about 关于 / account 账单 / arouse 唤起 |
| | ow | allow 允许 / brown 褐色的 / crowd 人群 |

| [ɔɪ] | 字母组合 | 例词 |
|---|---|---|
| | oi | avoid 避开 / broil 烤 / coin 硬币 / join 连接 |
| | oy | annoy 惹恼 / boy 男孩 / employ 雇用 |

## 元音 + r

元音（a, e, i, o, u）后面加上 r，发音变成 [ɑr]、[ɜ]、[ɚ]、[ɔr]。

| [ɑr] | 字母组合 | 例词 |
|---|---|---|
| | ar | are 是 / art 艺术 / card 纸牌 / hard 硬的 |

| | 字母组合 | 例　　词 |
|---|---|---|
| [ɜ] | er | certain 无疑的 / fertile 肥沃的 / her 她的 |
| | ir | bird 鸟 / dirt 灰尘 / first 第一的 / sir 先生 |
| | or | word 文字 / work 工作 / world 世界 |
| | ur | hurt 伤痛 / murder 谋杀 / return 回来 |

| | 字母组合 | 例　　词 |
|---|---|---|
| [ɚ] | ar | beggar 乞丐 / calendar 日历 / collar 衣领 |
| | er | after 在……之后 / anger 生气 / bother 打扰 |
| | or | actor 演员 / author 作者 / creator 创作者 |

| | 字母组合 | 例　　词 |
|---|---|---|
| [ɔr] | ar | war 战争 / ward 病房 / warm 温暖的 |
| | or | corn 玉米 / for 为了 / north 北方 / short 矮的 |

### 其他元音 + r

| | 字母组合 | 例　　词 |
|---|---|---|
| [ɛr] | air | affair 事件 / dairy 乳品店 / pair 一对 |
| | are | fare 票价 / hare 野兔 / parent 双亲 |
| | ear | bear 承担 / pear 梨 / swear 发誓 |
| | ere | there 在那里 / where 哪里 |

| | 字母组合 | 例　词 |
|---|---|---|
| [ɪr] | ear | appear 出现 / clear 干净的 / dear 亲爱的 |
| | ere | here 这里 / mere 仅仅的 / sincere 真诚的 |
| | eer | beer 啤酒 / career 职业 / cheer 欢呼 |

| | 字母组合 | 例　词 |
|---|---|---|
| [or] | oor | door 门 / floor 地板 |
| | ore | bore 使厌烦 |
| | our | four 四 |

## 不发音的辅音

| 字母组合 | 例　词 |
|---|---|
| mb（b 不发音） | bomb 炸弹 / climb 攀登 / comb 梳子 |
| h | honest 诚实的 / honor 荣誉 / hour 小时 |
| l | behalf 代表 / calf 小牛 / calm 冷静的 |
| t | ballet 芭蕾 / castle 城堡 / listen 聆听 |
| wr（w 不发音） | wrangle 争吵 / wrap 包装 / wrath 愤怒 |
| gn（g 不发音） | gnarl（树木）瘤 / gnash 气得咬牙 / gnat 小昆虫 / gnaw 咬、啃 / sign 记号 |
| gh（gh 不发音） | caught（catch 的过去式）抓到 / sigh 叹息 / through 经由 / tight 紧的 / weigh 称重 |
| kn（k 不发音） | knack 本领 / knee 膝盖 / knell 丧钟声 / knife 刀子 / knock 敲 / know 知道 |

| | |
|---|---|
| **pn**<br>（p 不发音） | pneumatic 空气的 / pneumonia 肺炎 |
| **ps**<br>（p 不发音） | pseudo 冒充的 / psychology 心理学 |
| **isl**<br>（s 不发音） | aisle 走道 / island 岛 |

## 混合辅音：字首组合

| 字母组合 | 发音 | 例　　词 |
|---|---|---|
| **bl** | [bl] | blank 空白的 / blend 混合 / blink 眨眼睛 |
| **br** | [br] | brain 头脑 / break 打破 / bridge 桥 |

| 字母组合 | 发音 | 例　　词 |
|---|---|---|
| **cl** | [kl] | clause 条款 / clever 聪明的 / cliff 悬崖 |
| **cr** | [kr] | crane 鹤 / cream 奶油 / crisis 危机 |

| 字母组合 | 发音 | 例　　词 |
|---|---|---|
| **dr** | [dr] | drama 戏剧 / dream 梦 / drizzle 下毛毛雨 |

| 字母组合 | 发音 | 例　　词 |
|---|---|---|
| **fl** | [fl] | flag 旗子 / flee 逃走 / flight 飞机班次 |
| **fr** | [fr] | fragile 脆弱的 / free 自由的 / friend 朋友 |

| 字母组合 | 发音 | 例　　词 |
|---|---|---|
| **gl** | [gl] | glad 快乐的 / gleam 微光 / glitter 闪烁 |
| **gr** | [gr] | grain 谷粒 / grey 灰色的 / grind 磨碎 |

| 字母组合 | 发音 | 例　　词 |
|---|---|---|
| pl | [pl] | plan 计划 / plea 恳求 / plot 阴谋 / plum 梅子 |
| pr | [pr] | pray 祈祷 / press 按 / private 私人的 |

sc / sk、sp、st 的组合为两个清辅音，第二个音要念成浊辅音：[sg]、[sb]、[sd]。

| 字母组合 | 发音 | 例　　词 |
|---|---|---|
| sc | [sk] | scale 规模 / scan 细看 / scoop 勺子 |
| sk | [sk] | sketch 素描 / ski 滑雪 / skin 皮肤 |
| sl | [sl] | slice 薄片 / slogan 口号 / slum 贫民区 |
| sm | [sm] | small 小的 / smell 闻 / smile 微笑 |
| sn | [sn] | sneeze 打喷嚏 / snicker 窃笑 / snuffle 鼻塞 |
| sp | [sp] | space 空间 / speed 速度 / spike 长钉 |
| st | [st] | state 状态 / steep 陡峭的 / step 步骤 |
| sw | [sw] | swallow 吞下 / sweat 流汗 / sweet 甜的 |
| scr | [skr] | scratch 搔 / scream 尖叫 / script 笔迹 |
| squ | [skw] | squad 小队 / square 广场 / squat 蹲下 |
| spl | [spl] | splice 粘接 / splinter 碎片 / split 使分离 |
| spr | [spr] | sprain 扭伤 / spray 喷洒 / spread 传播 |
| str | [str] | straw 稻草 / street 街道 / strength 力气 |

## 混合辅音：字尾组合

| 字母组合 | 发音 | 例　　词 |
|---|---|---|
| ct | [kt] | act 行动 / addict 使成瘾 / contact 接触 |
| ft | [ft] | swift 快速的 / theft 偷窃 / uplift 举起 |
| ld | [ld] | bold 大胆的 / child 孩童 / fold 折叠 |
| lf | [lf] | golf 高尔夫球 / gulf 海湾 / myself 我自己 |
| lm | [lm] | film 电影 / holm 河中沙洲 / palm 手掌 |
| lp | [lp] | alp 高山 / help 帮忙 / kelp 巨藻 |
| mp | [mp] | camp 露营 / dump 倾倒 / jump 跳 |
| nd | [nd] | almond 杏仁 / attend 出席 / band 乐团 |
| nk | [ŋk] | link 链接 / pink 粉红色 / prank 恶作剧 |
| nt | [nt] | blunt 直言不讳的 / grant 授予 / hint 暗示 |
| pt | [pt] | accept 接受 / attempt 企图 / concept 概念 |
| rd | [rd] | afford 买得起 / board 木板 / chord 和弦 |
| sk | [sk] | mask 面具 / risk 风险 / task 任务 |
| sp | [sp] | crisp 酥脆的 / gasp 喘气 / grasp 抓住 |
| st | [st] | adjust 调整 / artist 艺术家 / exist 存在 |

# Lesson 03 学习美国人的腔调与节奏

## 轻重音（Accent）

发音是学习外语的基础，在前面两节课讲解了自然发音的规则。读者在熟悉这些基本的发音规则后，相信已能够念出大部分常见的单词，并且轻松记住。

有了发音的基础之后，接下来要学习的就是轻重音（accent）了。轻重音是英语发音中非常重要的一环。重音是指要强调的音，目的是强调句子的重点以及表达的信息。举例来说，shorthand 这个词，如果念的时候把重音放在第一个音节，也就是 'shorthand，意思是"速记"；如果将重音放在 hand，也就是 short 'hand，意思就变成了"短的手"。另外一个例子是 blackbird 这个单词，如果念成 'blackbird，将重音放在第一个音节上，就是"北椋鸟"的意思，指一种鸟类；如果将重音放在 bird，念成了 black 'bird，则代表"黑色的鸟"。

由此可知，同一个单词，念的时候将轻重音放在不同音节上，会造成意思的差异，这点需要特别留意。

要练习轻重音，首先必须了解一个单词的轻重音、句子的重音与结构。每个句子里都会有一个或数个重音需要重读。需要重读的词发音较长，非重读的词发音较短且快。

分辨各个单词的重音位置非常重要。有些"双音节"单词由于重音位置的不同，可同时当作名词与动词，意思也有差异性。当名词时，通常重音在第一个音节；当动词时，重音在第二音节。

| 单词 | 名词 | 动词 |
|---|---|---|
| abstract | [ˈæbstrækt] 摘要 | [æbˈstrækt] 抽取 |
| conduct | [ˈkəndʌkt] 行为 | [kənˈdʌkt] 引导 |
| desert | [ˈdezərt] 沙漠 | [dɪˈzɜːt] 抛弃 |
| impact | [ˈɪmpækt] 冲击 | [ɪmˈpækt] 产生影响 |
| object | [ˈɑbdʒɛkt] 物体 | [əbˈdʒɛkt] 反对 |
| project | [ˈprɑdʒɛkt] 方案 | [prəˈdʒɛkt] 投射 |

接下来,我们来了解短语里的重音规则,大致上可分为下列五种:

**1. 所有格 + 名词→重音位于名词**
my bicycle → my 'bicycle

**2. 介词 + 名词→重音位于名词**
on the desk → on the 'desk

**3. 形容词 + 名词→重音位于名词**
a good idea → a good 'idea

**4. 副词 + 动词→重音位于动词**
slowly run → slowly 'run

**5. 动词 + 介词→重音位于介词**
go on → go 'on

接下来我们来了解句子里的重音。句子里需要重读的词通常是内容词(content words),内容词表达实质的内容,例如名词、动词与形容词等。不需重读的词通常是功能词(function words),例如冠词、介词、代词与连词等。

**例** 重读→内容词（content words）：
名　　词：book, movie, dog, desk, apple...
动　　词：go, run, sleep, make, eat...
形容词：good, bad, beautiful, black, white...

不需重读→功能词（function words）：
冠　　词：a, an, the...
介　　词：at, in, of...
代　　词：it, him, her, them, us...
连　　词：and, but...
助动词：do, will...

以下为范例，句子里画线部分是要强调的重点：
- It's a <u>good</u> idea.
- This is my <u>favorite book</u>.
- I <u>like</u> this <u>movie</u>.
- I <u>want</u> to <u>eat ice cream</u>.
- It's <u>not</u> my <u>business</u>.

综合上述要点，如果能熟悉单词、短语及句子的轻重音原则，便可掌握句子要传达的重点信息。有助于提高听力与口语水平，达到有效率的沟通。

## 语调（Intonation）

语调是一个句子的抑扬顿挫，可以表达出说话者的情绪，例如高兴、生气、悲伤、难过、怀疑……这是英语中非常重要的一部分。想要听得懂美国人所说的英语，除了要掌握基本的词汇量、分辨轻重音以外，语调也是不可或缺的元素。

中国学生在英语口语方面，虽然每个词都说得很清楚，却经常平铺直叙，忽略了句子所要表达的情绪，缺少语调的起伏与变化，导致句子没有抑扬顿挫，因此听起来不地道。

同样一个句子，语调不同，所表达的意思也会有所不同。语调的上升或下降，也会传达出不同的情绪，接下来看例子：

- I love swimming.

  I haven't seen you around.

  I have no idea.

  陈述的句子语调下降，表示信息结束。

- Are you sure?

  Do you like shopping?

  Is she your friend?

  疑问句语调上升，表示询问。

- You exercise every day, don't you?

  You exercise every day, don't you?

  这两句都是附加问句形态。第一句语调上升，表示不确定。第二句语调下降，表示肯定。

- What color do you like?

  Why did you do this?

  这两句都是 WH 问句，通常语调为下降，以了解信息。

- I'm sorry.

  I'm sorry?

  第一句是句号结尾，用于表达歉意，语调下降。而第二句以问号结尾，语调上升，是在听不清楚对方说话的时候，再次询问对方。

上述列举的英语语调范例。实际跟外国人对话时，会面临各种不同的语调变化。要能够听得懂并且对答如流，需要长时间接触大量的英语信息。读者可以收听英语广播、看英语电视剧、电影来训练听力；注意对话中的轻重音以及语调的变化，模仿外国人说话的语气。这些都有助于让你说英语说得更地道。

### 连音（Liaison）

美国人在说话上，除了加上重音以表达重点，另一个重要的部分便是连音。学会了连音，对于听力与口语都大有益处。我们可从五个要素来学习连音：

### 1. 缩音

美国人通常会将 be 动词与助动词缩减元音，以节省说话速度。例如：

- I am → I'm
- you are → you're
- they are → they're
- he is → he's
- I will → I'll
- she will → she'll
- I have → I've
- they have → they've

另外，否定的例子如下：

- is not → isn't
- was not → wasn't
- do not → don't
- does not → doesn't
- will not → won't
- have not → haven't
- cannot → can't

## 2. 弱音

弱音通常以功能词为主,例如冠词、介词、连词等,这些词在句子里不是那么重要,其元音通常被弱化成【ə】、【ʊ】,例如:

- was [wʌz] → [wəz]　　　　I was here.
- them [ðɛm] → [ðəm]　　　I don't like them.
- can [kæn] → [kən]　　　　I can do it.
- you [ju] → [jʊ]　　　　　　See you.
- to [tu] → [tʊ]　　　　　　　What did you say to him?
- of [ʌv] → [əv]　　　　　　　I'm thinking of you.
- for [fæ] → [fə]　　　　　　I did it for you.

## 3. 省音

以辅音结尾的词,下一个词如果开头是辅音时,通常会被省略不发声,但是舌头仍在发音位置上。

- Please give me a hand.
- I can't go.
- He broke the vase.
- I like black tea.
- Good morning.

## 4. 连音

句子里,如果单词结尾是辅音,而所接的单词开头是元音,便会产生连音的现象。

- Have a good day.
- I like it.
- Stand up.

- How can I help you?
- Please hold on a second.

## 5. 变音

有一些单词，由于结构不同，会产生变音的现象。

### (1)【sp】【st】【sk】念成【sb】【sd】【sg】
- 【sp】→【sb】space, special
- 【st】→【sd】student, stay
- 【sk】→【sg】skin, sky

### (2)【t】+【j】念成【tʃ】
- He set you up.
- I thought about you.

### (3)【d】+【j】念成【dʒ】
- Could you help me?
- I told you.

### (4)【s】+【j】念成【ʃ】
- I really miss you.
- Let me kiss you.

### (5)【z】+【j】念成【ʒ】
- Did you lose your mind?
- How was your weekend?

MEMO

# 美国人最常用的单词

## Part 2

# Lesson 04 add

[æd]

## 东西总是越加越多

💬 **add** 动词表示"增加、添加、相加、补充说明"。

- Would you please **add** up these numbers for me?
  可以请你帮我把这些数字加起来吗？　→ add up 表示"相加"

- Let's **add** Tabasco to the salsa!
  我们把塔巴斯科辣酱加到沙拉酱里吧！

- The teacher **added**, "We're going to have a quiz next week."
  老师补充说明："我们下周将有一个小考。"

- Please **add** some salt to the soup.
  请加一些盐在汤里。

- "I won't accept her apology," **added** Tim.
  提姆补了一句："我不接受她的道歉。"

---

**美国人常用短语**

- **add up** 相加
- **in order to** 为了
- **take a day off** 放假
- **be going to** 将要
- **rumor has it that** 据说

## 相关词汇群组记忆

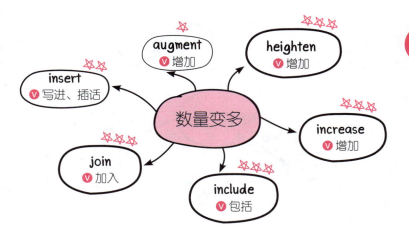

- **augment** [ɔgˈmɛnt] v 增加

  He tried to augment his income in order to buy a new house.
  为了买一栋新房子，他设法增加他的收入。

- **heighten** [ˈhaɪtn] v 增加

  A riot heightened the tension in the town.
  一场暴动增加了镇里的紧张气氛。　→ riot 表示"暴动"

- **increase** [ɪnˈkris] v 增加

  The approval rating of the mayor has been increasing.
  市长的满意度不断增加。

- **include** [ɪnˈklud] v 包括

  Everyone including me took a day off today.
  每个人今天都放假，包括我在内。

- **join** [dʒɔɪn] v 加入

  Does anyone want to join the study group?
  有人要加入读书会吗？

- **insert** [ɪnˈsɜrt] v 写进、插话

  Please insert your name in the blank.
  请在空白处写下你的名字。

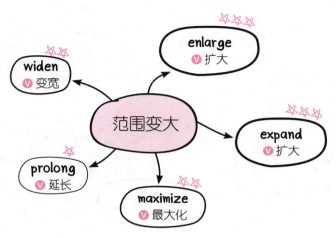

- **enlarge**
  [ɪn'lɑrdʒ]
  v 扩大

  Thousands of trees were planted to enlarge the green area in this city.
  这个城市种植了数千棵树，以扩大绿地。

- **expand**
  [ɪk'spænd]
  v 扩大

  You can expand your horizon by reading different kinds of books.
  阅读不同种类的书可扩展你的视野。

- **maximize**
  ['mæksɪmaɪz]
  v 最大化

  We must maximize our efforts to achieve the sales goal.
  我们必须尽最大的努力达到销售目标。

- **prolong**
  [prə'lɔŋ]
  v 延长

  Maintaining a healthy diet can prolong your life.
  维持健康饮食习惯可延长你的寿命。

- **widen**
  ['waɪdn]
  v 变宽

  The road widening construction in this area was under way.
  此区域的道路拓宽工程正在进行。
  → under way 表示"进行中的"

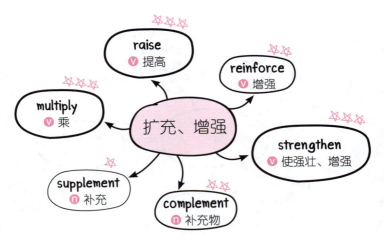

- **reinforce**
  [ˌriːɪnˈfɔːrs]
  ⓥ 增强

  After a car accident, his belief in God was reinforced.
  一次车祸后,他对上帝的信仰增强了。

- **strengthen**
  [ˈstreŋθn]
  ⓥ 使强壮、增强

  I do sit-ups every day to strengthen my abs.
  我每天做仰卧起坐以增强我的腹肌。　→ abs 表示"腹肌"

- **complement**
  [ˈkɑmplɪmənt]
  ⓝ 补充物

  The cream cheese is a perfect complement to the bagels.
  奶油乳酪是贝果的完美配料。

- **supplement**
  [ˈsʌplɪmənt]
  ⓝ 补充

  I took vitamins as a supplement to my diet.
  我把维生素作为饮食的补充。

- **multiply**
  [ˈmʌltɪplaɪ]
  ⓥ 乘

  Multiply one by one and you get one.
  一乘以一等于一。

- **raise**
  [reɪz]
  ⓥ 提高

  My salary has not been raised over the years.
  我的薪水已经很多年都没有增加了。

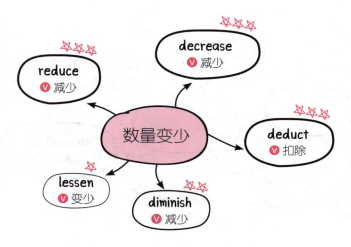

- **decrease**
  [dɪˈkris]
  ⓥ 减少

  The oil price has been decreasing.
  油价不断下跌。

- **deduct**
  [dɪˈdʌkt]
  ⓥ 扣除

  The parking fee was deducted from our bill.
  停车费已从我们的账单中扣除。

- **diminish**
  [dɪˈmɪnɪʃ]
  ⓥ 减少

  The El Nino effect on global climate has not diminished in recent years.
  厄尔尼诺现象对全球气候的效应近几年未曾减少。
  → El Nino 表示"厄尔尼诺现象"

- **lessen**
  [ˈlesn]
  ⓥ 变少

  After so many years, the impact of that car accident on him has lessened.
  这么多年后,那场车祸对他的影响已经减小了。

- **reduce**
  [rɪˈdus]
  ⓥ 减少

  Can you teach me how to reduce stress?
  你能教我如何减轻压力吗?

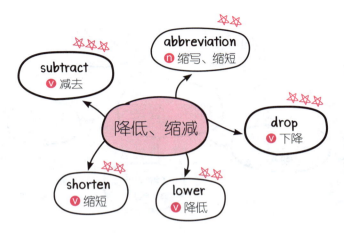

- **abbreviation**
  [ə,brivi'eɪʃn]
  n 缩写、缩短

  "OECD" is the abbreviation of Organization for Economic Cooperation and Development.
  "OECD"是经济合作与发展组织的缩写。

- **drop**
  [drɑp]
  v 下降

  In the desert, temperatures can drop to below zero degree Celsius at night.
  在沙漠，夜晚的温度会降到零摄氏度以下。
  → Celsius 表示"摄氏温度"

- **lower**
  ['loʊər]
  v 降低

  I asked my roommate to lower his voice.
  我要求室友降低音量。

- **shorten**
  ['ʃɔrtn]
  v 缩短

  This sentence needs to be shortened.
  这个句子必须缩短。

- **subtract**
  [səb'trækt]
  v 减去

  Subtract one from ten and you get nine.
  十减一等于九。

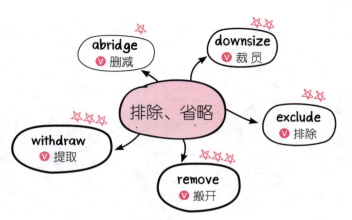

▶ **downsize**
['daʊnsaɪz]
v 裁员

Rumor has it that this company is going to downsize.
传闻这家公司将要裁员。 → rumor has it that 表示"据说……"

▶ **exclude**
[ɪk'sklud]
v 排除

The company excluded the possibility of the inside job.
公司已排除有内贼的可能性。

▶ **remove**
[rɪ'muv]
v 搬开

We removed the chairs to the garage.
我们将椅子搬到车库。

▶ **withdraw**
[wɪð'drɔ]
v 提取

I went to withdraw my money from the ATM today.
我今天去自动取款机取钱。

▶ **abridge**
[ə'brɪdʒ]
v 删减

The new script was abridged many times.
新剧本经过了多次删减。

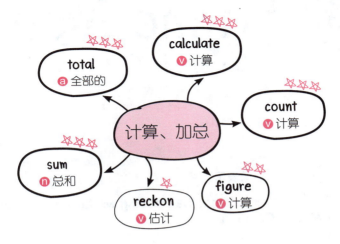

- **calculate**
  ['kælkjuleɪt]
  v 计算

  To control the budget, Bill is trying to calculate the cost of his wedding.
  为了控制预算，比尔尝试计算他婚礼的成本。

- **count**
  [kaʊnt]
  v 计算

  It's hard to count the numbers of the victims.
  受害者的人数难以计算。

- **figure**
  ['fɪgjɚ]
  v 计算

  We'd better figure the hours of using Internet per day.
  我们最好计算一下每天上网的时间。

- **reckon**
  ['rekən]
  v 估计

  I reckon that the concert ticket will cost me five hundred dollars.
  我估计演唱会门票将花掉我五百美元。

- **sum**
  [sʌm]
  n 总和

  What is the sum of one and one?
  一加一的总和是多少？

- **total**
  ['toʊtl]
  a 全部的

  What's the total amount of the sales?
  销售总额是多少？

# Lesson 05

# announce

[əˈnaʊns]

## 我有好消息要宣布

💬 announce 动词表示"宣布、宣告"。

- They announced that the wedding will take place at St. Patrick's Cathedral.
  他们宣布婚礼将在圣派翠克大教堂举行。 → take place 表示"举行"

- The organizer announced that the concert was called off due to the weather.
  主办单位宣布演唱会由于天气原因取消。 → call off 表示"取消"

- The government announced the water rationing policy.
  政府宣布了限水政策。 → rationing 表示"定量配给"

- His resignation hasn't been announced yet, and the manager is going to do it next Monday.
  他辞职一事尚未公布,经理将于下周一公布。

- They will announce the winner of the talent show after the votes have all been counted.
  在计算完票数后,他们将会公布才艺秀的优胜者。

### 美国人常用短语

- **simmer down** 冷静下来
- **take over** 接管
- **tell off** 斥责
- **put up with** 忍受

相关词汇群组记忆

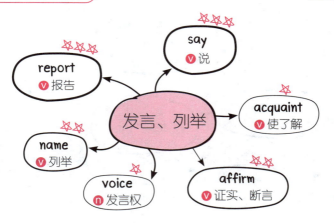

- **say**
  [seɪ]
  **v** 说

  Dylan said he just couldn't get over his ex-girlfriend.
  迪伦说他就是对前女友无法忘怀。→ get over 表示"忘怀"

- **acquaint**
  [əˈkweɪnt]
  **v** 使了解

  Our teacher acquainted us with the attendance rules.
  我们的老师让我们了解考勤规则。
  → acquaint with 表示"使……了解"

- **affirm**
  [əˈfɜrm]
  **v** 证实、断言

  The police affirmed that the bomber was shot dead on the spot.
  警方证实投弹者被当场击毙。

- **voice**
  [vɔɪs]
  **n** 发言权

  We don't have a voice in the decision making process.
  我们在决策过程中没有发言权。

- **name**
  [neɪm]
  **v** 列举

  I've been to many countries including Nepal, Peru, Chile, New Zealand, Spain and Venezuela, just to name a few.
  我去过很多国家,列举几个,包括尼泊尔、秘鲁、智利、新西兰、西班牙、委内瑞拉。

- **report**
  [rɪˈpɔrt]
  **v** 报告

  Make sure you report the progress to me.
  务必向我报告进度。

041

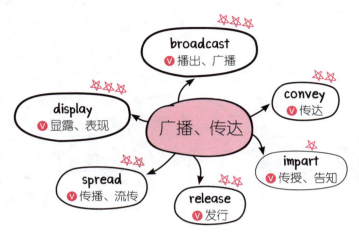

- **broadcast**
  ['brɔdkæst]
  v 播出、广播

  He has been broadcasting the weather for twenty years.
  他已经播报气象二十年了。

- **convey**
  [kən'veɪ]
  v 传达

  This article conveys the concept of globalization.
  这篇文章传达了全球化的概念。

- **impart**
  [ɪm'pɑrt]
  v 传授、告知

  I would love to impart my cooking skills to my students.
  我很乐意将我的烹饪技巧传授给我的学生。

- **release**
  [rɪ'lis]
  v 发行

  Did you check out the movie released yesterday?
  昨天上映的那部电影你看了吗? → check out 表示"看看"

- **spread**
  [sprɛd]
  v 传播、流传

  I'm going to find out who is spreading rumors about me.
  我打算查清楚是谁在散布关于我的谣言。

- **display**
  [dɪ'spleɪ]
  v 显露、表现

  He never displays his emotions to me.
  他从不在我面前显露他的情绪。

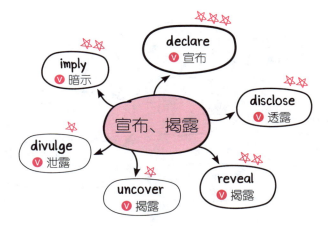

- **declare**
  [dɪˈkler]
  ⓥ 宣布

  He declared that he will retire next month.
  他宣布将于下个月退休。

- **disclose**
  [dɪsˈkloʊz]
  ⓥ 透露

  I won't disclose my secret to you.
  我不会向你透露我的秘密。

- **reveal**
  [rɪˈvil]
  ⓥ 揭露

  When can the mystery of Nessie be revealed?
  尼斯湖水怪之谜何时才能揭开？

- **uncover**
  [ʌnˈkʌvər]
  ⓥ 揭露

  Her continual embezzlement was finally uncovered after an investigation.
  经过调查，她持续挪用公款的行为终于被揭露。
  → embezzlement 表示"挪用公款"

- **divulge**
  [daɪˈvʌldʒ]
  ⓥ 泄露

  We were not allowed to divulge the details about the contract.
  我们不能泄露合约细节。

- **imply**
  [ɪmˈplaɪ]
  ⓥ 暗示

  Lisa tried to imply that I was biased against her.
  丽莎努力暗示我对她有偏见。
  → be biased against sb. 表示"对某人有偏见"

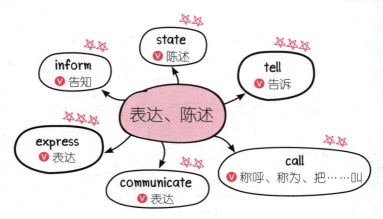

- **state**
  [steɪt]
  Ⓥ 陈述

  The doctor stated that there was no cure for his disease.
  医生表示他的疾病没有治疗方法。

- **tell**
  [tel]
  Ⓥ 告诉

  She told her son off for swearing.
  她斥责她的儿子说脏话。 → tell off 表示"斥责"

- **call**
  [kɔl]
  Ⓥ 称呼、称为、把……叫

  My friends always call me lazybones.
  我朋友总是叫我懒骨头。

- **communicate**
  [kə'mjunɪkeɪt]
  Ⓥ 表达

  I decided to communicate my anger to Craig.
  我决定向克雷格表达我的愤怒。

- **express**
  [ɪk'spres]
  Ⓥ 表达

  Why don't you simmer down and try to express your feelings?
  你为何不冷静下来,并试着表达你的感觉?
  → simmer down 表示"冷静下来"

- **inform**
  [ɪn'fɔrm]
  Ⓥ 告知

  The doctor informed me of Ted's condition.
  医生告知我泰德的病情。
  → inform sb. of sth. 表示"告知某人某事"

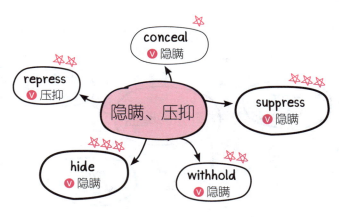

▶ **conceal**
[kən'sil]
Ⓥ 隐瞒

Did you conceal anything from me?
你向我隐瞒了什么事吗？

▶ **suppress**
[sə'prɛs]
Ⓥ 隐瞒

I believe that the government suppresses the truth about aliens.
我认为政府隐瞒了外星人的真相。

▶ **withhold**
[wɪð'hoʊld]
Ⓥ 隐瞒

Rebecca withheld the truth about her past from her husband.
蕾贝卡对她的丈夫隐瞒了她的往事。

▶ **hide**
[haɪd]
Ⓥ 隐瞒

I always hide my emotions.
我总是隐藏自己的情绪。

▶ **repress**
[rɪ'prɛs]
Ⓥ 压抑

Eric tried to repress his anxiety during a job interview.
艾瑞克在面试时努力压抑他的焦虑。
→ anxiety 表示"焦虑"

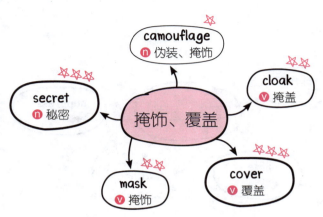

- **camouflage**
  ['kæməflɑʒ]
  **n** 伪装、掩饰

  Branches and leaves are often used as camouflage.
  树枝与树叶总被用来当作伪装。

- **cloak**
  [kloʊk]
  **v** 掩盖

  The whole city was cloaked in fog.
  整个城市被雾掩盖。

- **cover**
  ['kʌvər]
  **v** 覆盖

  Her bed was covered with rose petals.
  她的床铺满了玫瑰花瓣。

- **mask**
  [mæsk]
  **v** 掩饰

  I tried to mask my feelings.
  我试着掩饰我的感觉。

- **secret**
  ['sikrət]
  **n** 秘密

  Everyone has secrets deep down.
  每个人心底都有秘密。 → deep down 表示"在心底"

# become
[bɪˈkʌm]

## 事情总是变来变去

> become 动词表示"变成、成为、变得、适合"。

- It didn't take long before he became a well-known writer.
  没过多久他便成了一名知名作家。

- This city has become a hotbed of drug dealing.
  这座城市已成为毒品交易的温床。

- This skirt doesn't become me.
  这件裙子不适合我。

- After years and years of practice, he finally became a famous pianist.
  经过了许多年的苦心练习,他终于成了著名的钢琴家。

### 美国人常用短语

- **adjust to** 适应
- **go well** 进行顺利
- **be sick and tired of** 厌烦
- **abide by** 遵守
- **along the way** 一直以来
- **not have a clue** 不知道
- **concur with** 同意
- **go one's own way** 按照自己的意思行事

### 相关词汇群组记忆

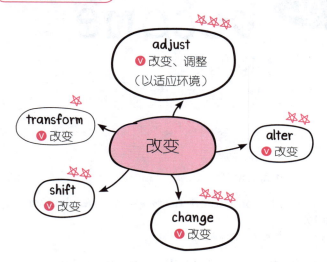

- **adjust**
  [ə'dʒʌst]
  Ⓥ 改变、调整（以适应环境）

  It's hard to adjust to different cultures.
  要适应不同的文化很困难。
  → adjust to 表示"适应"

- **alter**
  ['ɔltər]
  Ⓥ 改变

  The class schedule was altered many times.
  课程表已变更很多次了。

- **change**
  [tʃeɪndʒ]
  Ⓥ 改变

  The plan didn't go well, so we changed from plan A to plan B.
  计划进行不顺利，所以我们将A计划改成B计划。
  → go well 表示"进行顺利"

- **shift**
  [ʃɪft]
  Ⓥ 改变

  Her attitude toward upbringing shifted after getting married.
  她对教养的态度在结婚之后就改变了。

- **transform**
  [træns'fɔrm]
  Ⓥ 改变

  The basement of this building was transformed into a bar.
  这栋大楼的地下室被改装成了酒吧。

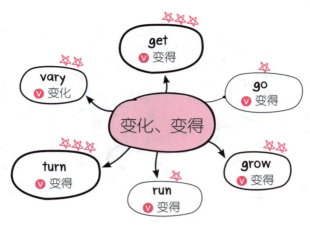

- **get**
  [gɛt]
  ⓥ 变得

  I'm getting sick and tired of your lies.
  我对你的谎言越来越厌烦。

- **go**
  [goʊ]
  ⓥ 变得

  I just want to know what went wrong.
  我只想知道什么出了问题。

- **grow**
  [groʊ]
  ⓥ 变得

  I'm growing to like this guy.
  我开始喜欢这个人了。

- **run**
  [rʌn]
  ⓥ 变得

  The well in the backyard was running dry.
  后院那口井变得干涸了。

- **turn**
  [tɜrn]
  ⓥ 变得

  Autumn is coming and leaves are turning yellow.
  秋天将至，树叶变黄了。

- **vary**
  ['veri]
  ⓥ 变化

  The price of this product varies from country to country.
  这个产品的价格各国间有所不同。

- ▶ **commence**
  [kə'mens]
  v 开始

  I commenced studying English last year.
  我从去年开始学英语。

- ▶ **develop**
  [dɪ'veləp]
  v 发展

  You should learn to develop your own interests.
  你应该学习培养自己的兴趣。

- ▶ **evolve**
  [i'vɑlv]
  v 发展、进化

  What did humans evolve from?
  人类是从什么进化而来的呢？

- ▶ **cultivate**
  ['kʌltɪveɪt]
  v 培养

  I decided to help my son to cultivate reading habits.
  我决定帮助我儿子培养阅读习惯。

- ▶ **modify**
  ['mɑdɪfaɪ]
  v 修改

  The conclusion of this essay needs to be modified.
  这篇短文的结尾需要修改。

- ▶ **advance**
  [əd'væns]
  v 进展

  Neuroscience has advanced rapidly in recent years.
  近几年神经科学发展迅速。

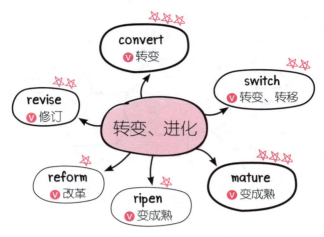

▶ **convert**
[kən'vɜrt]
v 转变

Elsa taught me how to convert a cardboard box into a decorative container.
艾莎教我怎么把纸箱变成装饰过的收纳盒。

▶ **switch**
[swɪtʃ]
v 转变、转移

Chris switched his attention to me.
克里斯将注意力转移到我身上。

▶ **mature**
[mə'tʃʊr]
v 变成熟

My writing skills fully matured after a lot of practice.
经过许多练习,我的写作技巧已完全成熟了。

▶ **ripen**
['raɪpən]
v 变成熟

Longan ripens in summer. It is my favorite fruit.
龙眼在夏季成熟,它是我最喜爱的水果。

▶ **reform**
[rɪ'fɔrm]
v 改革

We need to reform this old system.
我们必须改革这项旧的制度。

▶ **revise**
[rɪ'vaɪz]
v 修订

Most books need to be revised every few years.
大部分的书每隔几年都需要修订。

- **abide**
  [ə'baɪd]
  v 遵从

  Kate was disqualified for not abiding by the rules of the contest.
  凯特由于不遵守比赛规则而被取消了参赛资格。

- **consistent**
  [kən'sɪstənt]
  a 一致的

  My enthusiasm for my career has been consistent along the way.
  我对我事业的热忱一直没变过。
  → along the way 表示"一直以来"

- **continue**
  [kən'tɪnjuː]
  v 持续

  Sam will continue to go his own way no matter what.
  无论如何,山姆都将继续一意孤行。
  → go one's own way 表示"按照自己的意思行事"

- **last**
  [læst]
  v 持续

  The Chinese civilization has lasted for thousands of years.
  中华文明已持续了几千年之久。

- **remain**
  [rɪ'meɪn]
  v 保持

  I remained awake all night.
  我整晚都醒着。

- **stay**
  [steɪ]
  v 维持

  I don't have a clue why she stays angry all the time.
  我不知道为什么她总是气呼呼的。

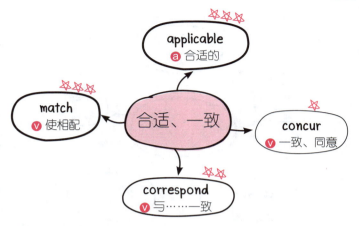

- **applicable**
  [əˈplɪkəbl]
  @ 合适的

  This application form is applicable to all students.
  这张申请表适用于所有学生。

- **concur**
  [kənˈkɜr]
  ⓥ 一致、同意

  I don't concur with you on this issue.
  在这个问题上，我不同意你的看法。
  → concur with 表示"同意"

- **correspond**
  [ˌkɔrəˈspɑnd]
  ⓥ 与……一致

  His facial expressions don't always correspond with his true emotions.
  他的脸部表情不一定与他真实的情感一致。
  → correspond with 表示"符合"

- **match**
  [mætʃ]
  ⓥ 使相配

  Your handbag matches your high heels.
  你的包很配你的高跟鞋。

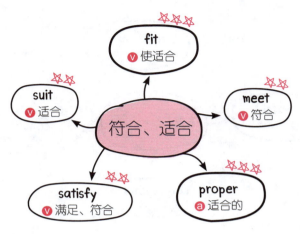

▶ **fit**
[fɪt]
ⓥ 使适合

This dress fits me well.
这件连衣裙很适合我。

▶ **meet**
[mit]
ⓥ 符合

Your test scores do not meet the requirement.
你的测验成绩不符合要求。

▶ **proper**
['prɑ:pər]
ⓐ 适合的

Picking your nose in public is not a proper thing to do.
当众挖鼻孔并不恰当。

▶ **satisfy**
['sætɪsfaɪ]
ⓥ 满足、符合

Satisfying customers' needs is the top priority of our company.
满足顾客需求是我们公司最优先考量的事项。
→ priority 表示 "优先考虑事项"

▶ **suit**
[sut]
ⓥ 适合

Please let me know what time suits you best for the meeting.
请让我知道什么时间最适合你开会吧。

# Lesson 07

# best

[best]

## 多多赞美与鼓励吧

> best 形容词表示"最好的、主要的、最合适的";
> 副词表示"最好地、最合适地";
> 名词表示"最好、最大努力"。

- The Wave in Arizona is one of the best photo locations.
  亚利桑那州的"波浪岩"是最好的拍照地点之一。

- What do you like best about this book?
  你最喜欢这本书的哪些地方?

- I'll do my best on this project. I won't let you down.
  我会尽全力完成这项计划,不会让你失望的。
  → let sb. down 表示"使某人失望"

- She is my best friend; there are no secrets between us.
  她是我最好的朋友,我们之间没有秘密。

- This is the best movie I have ever seen.
  这是我看过的最好看的电影了。

### 美国人常用短语

- **put on** 举办(演出)
- **bring up** 提出
- **crack sb. up** 令人捧腹大笑
- **cheat on sb.** 对……不忠

相关词汇群组记忆

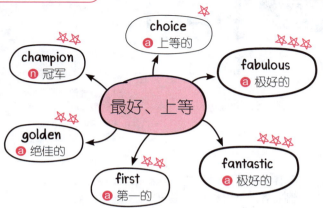

- **choice**
  [tʃɔɪs]
  ⓐ 上等的

  We provide plenty of choice products at fair prices in our store.
  我们的店里提供许多价格合理的高品质产品。

- **fabulous**
  ['fæbjələs]
  ⓐ 极好的

  Your idea sounds fabulous!
  你的主意听起来很棒!

- **fantastic**
  [fæn'tæstɪk]
  ⓐ 极好的

  You've got a promotion! That's fantastic!
  你升迁了!真是太好了!

- **first**
  [fɜrst]
  ⓐ 第一的

  William was the first runner to cross the finish line in this race.
  威廉是这场比赛中第一个越过终点线的赛跑者。

- **golden**
  ['goʊldən]
  ⓐ 绝佳的

  This is your golden opportunity to broaden your working experience.
  这是你拓展工作经验的绝佳机会。

- **champion**
  ['tʃæmpiən]
  ⓝ 冠军

  Who's going to be the champion of this competition?
  谁将是赢得这场竞赛的冠军?

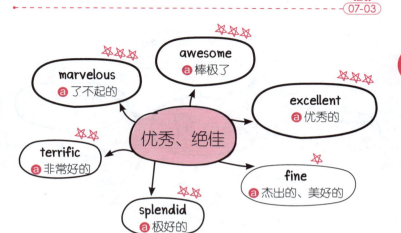

▶**awesome**
['ɔsəm]
ⓐ 棒极了

That movie was really awesome!
那部电影真的很棒!

▶**excellent**
['eksələnt]
ⓐ 优秀的

Our school's volleyball team has done an excellent job today.
我们学校的排球队今天表现得很优秀。

▶**fine**
[faɪn]
ⓐ 杰出的、美好的

We should learn to appreciate fine art.
我们应该学习欣赏杰出艺术作品。

▶**splendid**
['splendɪd]
ⓐ 极好的

These paintings are just splendid.
这些画真的很美。

▶**terrific**
[tə'rɪfɪk]
ⓐ 非常好的

This show was terrific! It was worth every penny.
这场表演太棒了!非常值得。

▶**marvelous**
['mɑrvələs]
ⓐ 了不起的

This room has a marvelous window view.
这个房间有很棒的窗景。

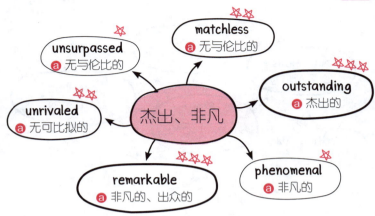

- **matchless**
  ['mætʃləs]
  ⓐ 无与伦比的

  She has matchless culinary skills.
  她有无人能比的烹饪技术。→ culinary 表示"烹饪的"

- **outstanding**
  [aʊt'stændɪŋ]
  ⓐ 杰出的

  Virginia Woolf is one of the most outstanding feminist writers.
  弗吉尼亚·伍尔芙是最杰出的女性主义作家之一。

- **phenomenal**
  [fə'nɑmɪnl]
  ⓐ 非凡的

  Our synchronized swimming team put on a phenomenal performance tonight.
  我们的花样游泳队今晚带来了一场非常精彩的演出。

- **remarkable**
  [rɪ'mɑrkəbl]
  ⓐ 非凡的、出众的

  Tennessee Williams was a remarkable playwright. *A Streetcar Named Desire* is one of his most famous works.
  田纳西·威廉斯是一名杰出的剧作家。《欲望号街车》是他最有名的作品之一。

- **unrivaled**
  [ʌn'raɪvld]
  ⓐ 无可比拟的

  He is a man of unrivaled talents.
  他是一个无比有才华的人。

- **unsurpassed**
  [ˌʌnsər'pæst]
  ⓐ 无与伦比的

  It is his unsurpassed intelligence that makes him outstanding.
  他无与伦比的聪明才智使他非常杰出。

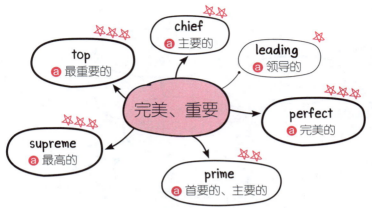

- **chief**
 [tʃif]
 ⓐ 主要的

 The chief goal of this class is to build your writing skills.
 这堂课的主要目标是增进你的写作技巧。

- **leading**
 [ˈlidɪŋ]
 ⓐ 领导的

 Our company has been the leading manufacturer in LED.
 我们的公司一直以来都是 LED 的领导厂商。

- **perfect**
 [ˈpɜrfɪkt]
 ⓐ 完美的

 This is my dream house. It's so perfect.
 这就是我梦想中的房屋，真的很完美。

- **prime**
 [praɪm]
 ⓐ 首要的、主要的

 A soldier's prime duty is to obey.
 士兵的首要义务是服从。

- **supreme**
 [suˈprim]
 ⓐ 最高的

 The Supreme Court is the highest federal court in the USA.
 美国联邦最高法院是美国最高级别的联邦法院。

- **top**
 [tɑp]
 ⓐ 最重要的

 Children's education is my top concern.
 儿童教育是我首要考虑的事。

059

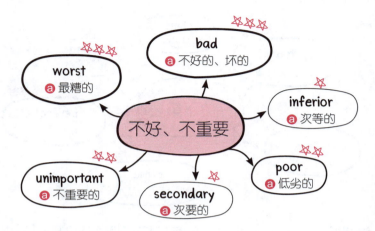

- **bad**
  [bæd]
  @ 不好的、坏的

  Breaking bad habits is easier said than done.
  改掉坏习惯是说比做容易。
  → easier said than done 表示"说比做容易"

- **inferior**
  [ɪnˈfɪriər]
  @ 次等的

  Never think you are inferior to anyone.
  绝不要认为你不如别人。

- **poor**
  [pɔr]
  @ 低劣的

  These tea cups are of poor quality.
  这些茶杯质量不好。

- **secondary**
  [ˈsekənderi]
  @ 次要的

  Your opinions are just secondary.
  你的意见不是那么重要。

- **unimportant**
  [ˌʌnɪmˈpɔːrtnt]
  @ 不重要的

  I pay no attention to those unimportant things.
  我不关心那些不重要的事情。

- **worst**
  [wɜrst]
  @ 最糟的

  Silence is the worst way of communication.
  沉默是最糟的沟通方式。

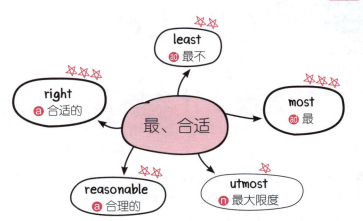

▶ **least**
[list]
ad 最不

Jeffrey may be the least humorous person I've ever met.
杰弗里可能是我遇见过最没幽默感的人了。

▶ **most**
[moʊst]
ad 最

This was the most hilarious movie I've ever seen. It really cracked me up.
这是我看过最搞笑的电影了,简直令我捧腹大笑。
→ crack sb. up 表示"令人捧腹大笑"

▶ **utmost**
[ˈʌtmoʊst]
n 最大限度

I will do my utmost to help those who are in need of help.
我会尽力去帮助需要帮助的人们。

▶ **reasonable**
[ˈriznəbl]
a 合理的

Your reason for cheating on your wife doesn't sound reasonable.
你对妻子不忠的理由听起来不合理。
→ cheat on sb. 表示"对……不忠"

▶ **right**
[raɪt]
a 合适的

I'm sure Joe is the right person for the role.
我确信乔是这个角色的适当人选。

## Lesson 08

# concern

[kən'sɜrn]

## 都关心些什么事呢

> **concern** 动词表示"使关心、使忧虑、影响到、关系到";名词表示"关心、关心的事"。

- My sister came down with the flu and I was concerned about her.

  我妹妹感冒了,我很担心她。 → come down with 表示"染……病"

- This magazine is concerned with the current political situation.

  这本杂志的内容是关于当前政治形势的。

- When it comes to travel, money is my main concern.

  一谈到旅行,钱是我主要关心的事。

- It is no concern of yours. Back off.

  这跟你一点关系都没有,少烦我。 → back off 表示"走开、别烦我"

- Stop eating junk food. I'm a bit concerned about your health.

  不要再吃垃圾食物了,我有点担心你的健康状况。

**美国人常用短语**

- **take heed of** 注意
- **fender-bender** 小车祸
- **blow off steam** 宣泄压力
- **shrug off** 对……置之不理

相关词汇群组记忆 08-02

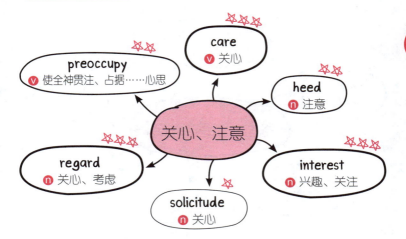

- ▶ **care**
  [kɛr]
  ⓥ 关心

  I really care about the children's education in remote communities.
  我非常关心偏远地区的儿童教育情况。

- ▶ **heed**
  [hid]
  ⓝ 注意

  Iris took no heed of her mother's advice.
  艾莉丝不注意她妈妈的建议。 → take heed of 表示"注意"

- ▶ **interest**
  ['ɪntrəst]
  ⓝ 兴趣、关注

  He has great interest in various serial murder cases.
  他对各种连环谋杀案有极大的兴趣。

- ▶ **solicitude**
  [sə'lɪsɪtud]
  ⓝ 关心

  Parents always show their solicitude for their children.
  父母总是表现出对他们小孩的关心。

- ▶ **regard**
  [rɪ'gɑrd]
  ⓝ 关心、考虑

  She pays no regard to her family's feelings.
  她没有考虑到她家人的感受。

- ▶ **preoccupy**
  [pri'ɑkjupaɪ]
  ⓥ 使全神贯注、占据……心思

  These unsolved problems keep preoccupying me.
  这些未解的问题一直占据着我的心思。

063

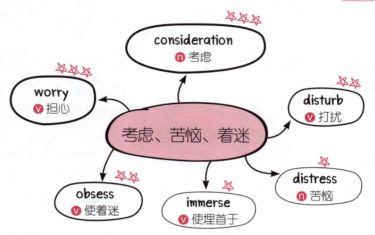

- **consideration**
  [kən͵sɪdə'reɪʃn]
  n 考虑

  Thank you for your careful consideration.
  谢谢你的详细考虑。

- **disturb**
  [dɪ'stɜrb]
  v 打扰

  Emma hung a sign saying "Do not disturb" on her door.
  艾玛在她房间门上挂上了一个写着"请勿打扰"的标志。

- **distress**
  [dɪ'stres]
  n 苦恼

  The illness caused him so much distress.
  疾病带给他很多痛苦。

- **immerse**
  [ɪ'mɜrs]
  v 使埋首于

  I've been immersed in writing my book for several months.
  有好几个月的时间,我都埋头写我的书。

- **obsess**
  [əb'ses]
  v 使着迷

  I don't know why Mark is so obsessed with Bridget.
  我不知道马克为什么对布丽琪这么着迷。

- **worry**
  ['wɜri]
  v 担心

  I had a car accident this morning. Don't worry. It was just a fender-bender.
  我今天早上发生了车祸,但别担心,只是小擦碰而已。
  → fender-bender 表示"小车祸"

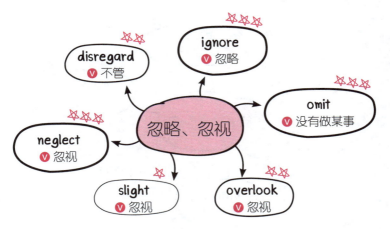

- **ignore**
  [ɪgˈnɔr]
  **v** 忽略

  Kyle decided to ignore all the reviews about his new book.
  凯尔决定忽略关于他新书的所有评论。

- **omit**
  [əˈmɪt]
  **v** 没有做某事

  Daniel omitted to tell his wife he wouldn't make it home for dinner.
  丹尼尔没有告诉他的妻子他来不及回家吃晚餐。

- **overlook**
  [ˌoʊvərˈlʊk]
  **v** 忽视

  I made a mistake because I overlooked an important detail.
  我因为忽略了一个重要细节而犯了一个错误。

- **slight**
  [slaɪt]
  **v** 忽视

  I felt slighted because he didn't talk to me.
  我觉得自己被冷落了，因为他不跟我讲话。

- **neglect**
  [nɪˈglɛkt]
  **v** 忽视

  My father never neglects his health. He has a check-up every year.
  我父亲从不忽视他的健康，他每年都做健康检查。
  → check-up 表示"健康检查"

- **disregard**
  [ˌdɪsrɪˈgɑrd]
  **v** 不管

  Anna disregards all the criticism about her.
  安娜不理会所有关于她的批评。

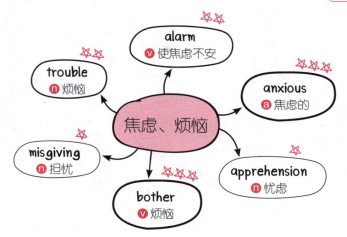

- **alarm**
  [ə'lɑrm]
  **v** 使焦虑不安

  A strange noise alarmed me.
  一个奇怪的声响令我感到不安。

- **anxious**
  ['æŋkʃəs]
  **a** 焦虑的

  I'm so anxious and angry right now. I need a place to blow off steam.
  我现在非常焦虑和生气，我需要一个地方宣泄压力。
  → blow off steam 表示"宣泄压力"

- **apprehension**
  [ˌæprɪ'henʃn]
  **n** 忧虑

  People in this country live in apprehension and fear.
  这个国家的人们生活在忧虑与恐惧中。

- **bother**
  ['bɑðər]
  **v** 烦恼

  I had a toothache and it really bothered me.
  我牙齿疼，真的令我很烦。

- **misgiving**
  [ˌmɪs'gɪvɪŋ]
  **n** 担忧

  Many people have serious misgivings about abolishing the death penalty.
  很多人对于废除死刑深感疑虑。
  → abolish 表示"废除"；penalty 表示"刑罚"

- **trouble**
  ['trʌbl]
  **n** 烦恼

  I hope I can shrug off all my troubles.
  我希望自己可以对所有的烦恼都置之不理。
  → shrug off 表示"对……置之不理"

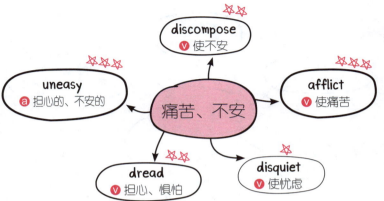

- **discompose**
 [ˌdɪskəm'poʊz]
 v 使不安

 A stranger was following me and this discomposed me.
 有一个陌生人跟着我，令我不安。

- **afflict**
 [ə'flɪkt]
 v 使痛苦

 His wife's death afflicted him so much.
 他的妻子的死使他非常痛苦。

- **disquiet**
 [dɪs'kwaɪət]
 v 使忧虑

 His silence disquieted me.
 他的沉默令我焦虑不安。

- **dread**
 [drɛd]
 v 担心、惧怕

 Albert dreads to meet his ex-wife.
 艾伯特害怕遇到他的前妻。

- **uneasy**
 [ʌn'izi]
 a 担心的、不安的

 He was uneasy about the hostage's safety.
 他为人质的安全感到不安。

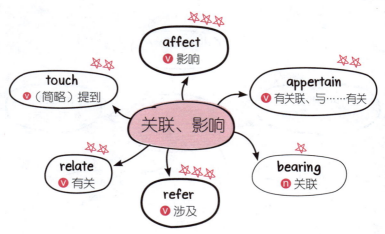

- **affect**
  [əˈfekt]
  v 影响

  There has been no rainfall for a long time. All crops were affected by the drought.
  已经很久没有下雨了。所有的作物都受到了干旱的影响。

- **appertain**
  [ˌæpərˈteɪn]
  v 有关联、与……有关

  Art appreciation ability appertains to aesthetic experience.
  艺术鉴赏能力与美感经验有关。 → aesthetic 表示"美学的"

- **bearing**
  [ˈberɪŋ]
  n 关联

  Psychological health has a bearing on physical health.
  心理健康与身体健康有关联。

- **refer**
  [rɪˈfɜr]
  v 涉及

  This movie referred to the Bible.
  这部电影内容与圣经有关。 → refer to 表示"涉及"

- **relate**
  [rɪˈleɪt]
  v 有关

  I believe that most diseases are related to stress.
  我认为大部分疾病都与压力有关。

- **touch**
  [tʌtʃ]
  v （简略）提到

  This novel touched on the witch-hunt in the Middle Ages.
  这部小说简单提到中世纪时期的猎巫行动。

# Lesson 09

# decide

[dɪˈsaɪd]

## 做决定真的不容易

**decide** 动词表示"决定"。

- I **decided** to buy a new air conditioner.
  我决定买一台新的空调。

- It's hard to **decide** which restaurant is my favorite.
  很难决定哪间餐厅才是我最喜爱的。

- Anita **decided** to move down south.
  安妮塔决定搬到南部。

- I've **decided** to quit my job, because I can see no future in it.
  我决定辞职,因为我觉得这个工作没有前途。

- The location for this event is **decided**.
  这个活动的地点已经定了。

### 美国人常用短语

- **on the same page** 意见一致
- **chew over** 仔细考虑
- **mull over** 仔细考虑
- **pick and choose** 东挑西拣
- **single out** 挑出、选出
- **think through** 彻底想清楚
- **weigh up** 权衡

### 相关词汇群组记忆

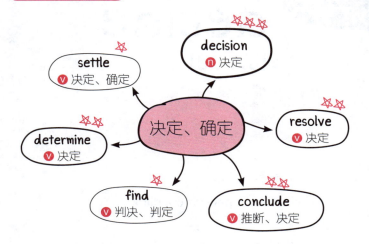

▶ **decision**
[dɪˈsɪʒən]
n 决定

This is really a tough decision.
这真是一个困难的决定。

▶ **resolve**
[rɪˈzɑlv]
v 决定

Kelly resolved to file a lawsuit against this company.
凯莉决定对这家公司提起诉讼。

▶ **conclude**
[kənˈklud]
v 推断、决定

We concluded that the mission failed.
我们推断任务失败了。

▶ **find**
[faɪnd]
v 判决、判定

The suspect was found not guilty and was released by the court.
嫌犯被判无罪并且当庭释放。　→ suspect 表示"嫌疑犯"

▶ **determine**
[dɪˈtɜrmɪn]
v 决定

Nancy finally determined to lose weight for health reasons.
为了健康，南希终于决定要减肥。

▶ **settle**
[ˈsetl]
v 决定、确定

Our travel plan to Europe was all settled.
我们的欧洲旅行计划已经都确定了。

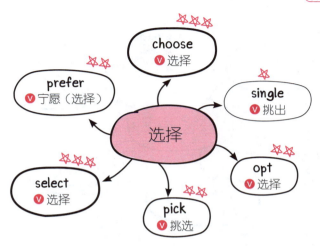

▶ **choose**
[tʃuz]
Ⓥ 选择

Phoebe chose journalism as her major.
菲比选择新闻学作为她的主修科目。

▶ **single**
['sɪŋɡl]
Ⓥ 挑出

The manager singled him out for his efforts.
经理特别提出他的努力。 → single out 表示"挑出、选出"

▶ **opt**
[ɑpt]
Ⓥ 选择

Carolyn opted to be a teacher after graduation.
卡洛琳毕业后选择当一名教师。

▶ **pick**
[pɪk]
Ⓥ 挑选

She loves to pick and choose at the food market.
她爱在菜市场东挑西拣。 → pick and choose 表示"东挑西拣"

▶ **select**
[sɪ'lɛkt]
Ⓥ 选择

I have no idea about how to select a good restaurant.
我不知道如何选择一家好的餐厅。

▶ **prefer**
[prɪ'fɝ]
Ⓥ 宁愿（选择）

I'm not a social person. I prefer a quiet place to live.
我不是一个爱热闹的人。我宁愿住在安静的地方。

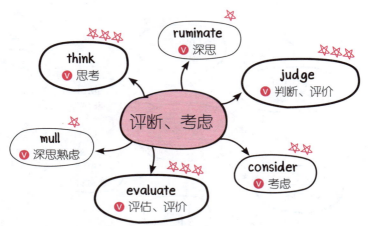

- ▶ **ruminate**
  ['ruːmɪneɪt]
  Ⓥ 深思

  I kept ruminating about what he said to me.
  我不停地思考他对我说的话。

- ▶ **judge**
  [dʒʌdʒ]
  Ⓥ 判断、评价

  Don't judge me like that. It's not fair.
  别那样评判我，这不公平。

- ▶ **consider**
  [kən'sɪdər]
  Ⓥ 考虑

  She is considering apologizing to her mother.
  她正在考虑向她的母亲道歉。

- ▶ **evaluate**
  [ɪ'væljueɪt]
  Ⓥ 评估、评价

  The practicability of this project needs to be evaluated carefully.
  这个计划的可行性需要经过审慎的评估。

- ▶ **mull**
  [mʌl]
  Ⓥ 深思熟虑

  I've been mulling over his proposal for several weeks.
  我这几个星期都在仔细思考他的提议。
  → mull over 表示"仔细考虑"

- ▶ **think**
  [θɪŋk]
  Ⓥ 思考

  I've thought through all the possible answers to this question.
  我已经彻底思考过这个问题的所有可能性答案了。

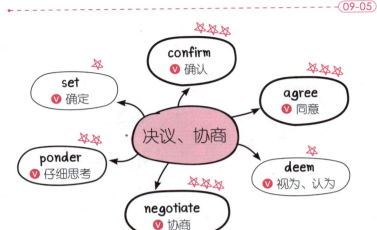

- **confirm**
  [kən'fɜrm]
  Ⓥ 确认

  I need to confirm some information about the reservation with you.
  我需要与你确认一些预订资料。

- **agree**
  [ə'gri]
  Ⓥ 同意

  I totally agree with him. We are on the same page.
  我完全同意他。我们意见一致。

- **deem**
  [dim]
  Ⓥ 视为、认为

  Perseverance is deemed to be the key to success.
  不屈不挠的精神被视为是成功的关键。
  → perseverance 表示"毅力、不屈不挠的精神"

- **negotiate**
  [nɪ'goʊʃieɪt]
  Ⓥ 协商

  Our company is trying to negotiate with the rival company.
  我们的公司正设法与敌对公司协商。

- **ponder**
  ['pɑndər]
  Ⓥ 仔细思考

  The ethical issues of human cloning need to be pondered over.
  克隆人的伦理问题必须仔细思考。

- **set**
  [sɛt]
  Ⓥ 确定

  The start date of the fall semester has been set.
  秋季学期开学日已经确定。

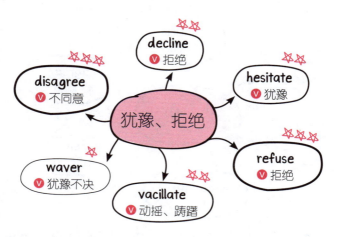

- **decline**
 [dɪˈklaɪn]
 v 拒绝

 I don't know why he **declined** this role.
 我不知道他为什么拒绝出演这个角色。

- **hesitate**
 [ˈhezɪteɪt]
 v 犹豫

 Lily is still **hesitating** about her boyfriend's proposal.
 莉莉对她男友的求婚仍感到犹豫。

- **refuse**
 [rɪˈfjuz]
 v 拒绝

 I **refuse** to accept your offer.
 我拒绝接受你的提议。

- **vacillate**
 [ˈvæsəleɪt]
 v 动摇、踌躇

 He always **vacillates** between the ideal and the reality.
 他总是在理想与现实之间犹豫不定。

- **waver**
 [ˈweɪvər]
 v 犹豫不决

 He has been **wavering** between buying a new car and a second-hand car.
 他很犹豫要买新车还是二手车。

- **disagree**
 [ˌdɪsəˈgri]
 v 不同意

 I strongly **disagree** with you on this issue.
 我在这个问题上坚决不同意你的看法。

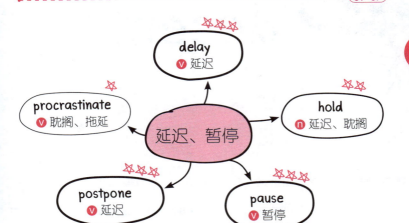

- **delay**
  [dɪˈleɪ]
  v 延迟

  They delayed the wedding until next year.
  他们将婚礼延期到明年。

- **hold**
  [hoʊld]
  n 延迟、耽搁

  The concert was put on hold for almost two hours.
  演唱会延迟了将近两个小时。

- **pause**
  [pɔːz]
  v 暂停

  The speaker paused because someone interrupted him.
  演讲者停顿下来，因为有人打断他说话。

- **postpone**
  [poʊˈspoʊn]
  v 延迟

  Today's meeting was postponed until next month.
  今天的会议延期到下个月。

- **procrastinate**
  [proʊˈkræstɪneɪt]
  v 耽搁、拖延

  Debby works hard and never procrastinates.
  黛比认真工作，而且从不拖延。

# Lesson 10

# decent
['disnt]

## 行为与举止要得体

**decent** 形容词表示"像样的、正派的、得体的、适当的"。

- It's hard to find a decent house around this neighborhood.
  在这片街区很难找到像样的房子。

- You are by no means a decent man.
  你不是个正派的人。 → by no means 表示"一点也不"

- The judge gave him a decent sentence.
  法官对他做出了合理的判决。

- He's a decent person. He never takes advantage of others.
  他是一个正派的人,从来不占别人便宜。

- You should wear something decent for the wedding. Flip-flops are not an option.
  参加婚礼要穿得体一点,绝对不可以穿人字拖鞋。

**美国人常用短语**
- **by no means** 一点也不
- **judge a book by its cover** 以貌取人
- **from time to time** 偶尔
- **make up one's mind** 下定决心

相关词汇群组记忆　　10-02

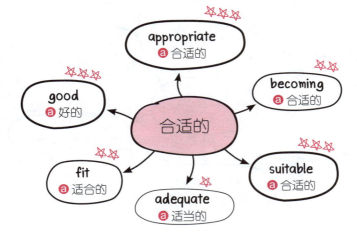

▶ **appropriate**
[ə'proʊpriət]
ⓐ 合适的

Burping loudly in public is not appropriate.
当众大声打嗝并不恰当。　→ burp 表示"打嗝"

▶ **becoming**
[bɪ'kʌmɪŋ]
ⓐ 合适的

The new haircut is becoming for you.
新发型很适合你。

▶ **suitable**
['sutəbl]
ⓐ 合适的

I think I'm not suitable for being a teacher.
我想我不适合当老师。

▶ **adequate**
['ædɪkwət]
ⓐ 适当的

We don't think that the current welfare policies are adequate to meet people's needs.
我们认为目前福利政策不符合人们的需求。

▶ **fit**
[fɪt]
ⓐ 适合的

This colorful table cloth is fit for the dining table.
这块鲜艳的桌布很适合这张餐桌。

▶ **good**
[gʊd]
ⓐ 好的

Mandy made up her mind to do a good deed every day.
曼蒂下定决心要每天做一件好事。

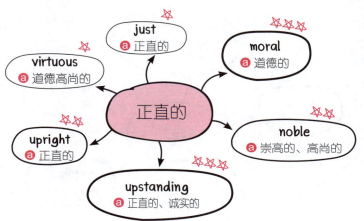

- **just**
  [dʒʌst]
  ⓐ 正直的

  My friend Baron is completely a just man.
  我的朋友贝伦是一个十分正直的人。

- **moral**
  ['mɔrəl]
  ⓐ 道德的

  I do everything abiding by moral principles.
  我行事遵从道德原则。→ abide by 表示"遵守"

- **noble**
  ['noʊbl]
  ⓐ 崇高的、高尚的

  Would you fight for a noble cause?
  你会为了崇高的理念而奋斗吗?

- **upstanding**
  [ˌʌp'stændɪŋ]
  ⓐ 正直的、诚实的

  Mr. Darcy is an upstanding and self-disciplined man. That's what I like about him.
  达西先生是个正直且自律的人,这就是我喜欢他的地方。

- **upright**
  ['ʌpraɪt]
  ⓐ 正直的

  How could an upright man like him commit a crime?
  像他这么正直的人怎么会犯罪呢?

- **virtuous**
  ['vɜrtʃuəs]
  ⓐ 道德高尚的

  Even a virtuous person can make a mistake from time to time.
  即使是道德高尚的人也会偶尔犯错。

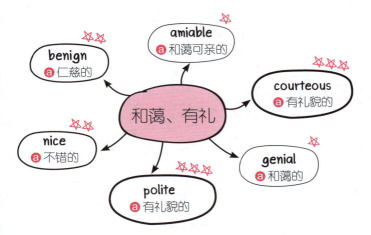

- **amiable**
  ['eɪmɪəbl]
  @ 和蔼可亲的

  I don't believe he is an amiable man because he looks so serious.
  我不相信他是一个和蔼可亲的人，因为他看起来很严肃。

- **courteous**
  ['kɜrtɪəs]
  @ 有礼貌的

  That young man is very gentle and courteous. He greets everyone with a smile.
  那位年轻人非常温和有礼貌，他对每个人都以笑脸相迎。

- **genial**
  ['dʒinɪəl]
  @ 和蔼的

  My mother is very genial and kind. She gives me a hug every day.
  我母亲非常和蔼亲切。她每天都给我一个拥抱。

- **polite**
  [pə'laɪt]
  @ 有礼貌的

  She was trying very hard to be polite.
  她非常努力要表现得有礼貌。

- **nice**
  [naɪs]
  @ 不错的

  This coat looks nice on you.
  你穿这件外套很好看。

- **benign**
  [bɪ'naɪn]
  @ 仁慈的

  My grandmother is such a benign person. She loves to help people.
  我的祖母非常仁慈，乐于帮助别人。

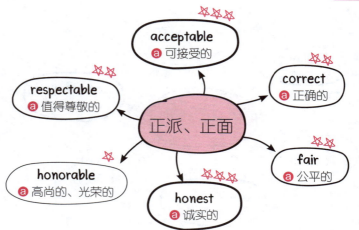

- **acceptable**
  [ək'septəbl]
  @ 可接受的

  The newly designed courses are acceptable.
  新规划的课程尚可接受。

- **correct**
  [kə'rekt]
  @ 正确的

  Please circle the correct answer.
  请圈出正确答案。

- **fair**
  [fer]
  @ 公平的

  It is not fair to judge a book by its cover.
  以貌取人并不公平。
  → judge a book by its cover 表示"以貌取人"

- **honest**
  ['ɑnɪst]
  @ 诚实的

  To be honest, I'm a cynical person through and through.
  老实说,我是个彻头彻尾愤世嫉俗的人。

- **honorable**
  ['ɑnərəbəl]
  @ 高尚的、光荣的

  Many soldiers sacrificed their lives and died for an honorable cause.
  许多士兵牺牲生命,为了高尚的理念而死去。

- **respectable**
  [rɪ'spektəbl]
  @ 值得尊敬的

  Jonathan is a respectable man. He never speaks ill of others.
  强纳森是一个值得尊敬的人。他从不说别人坏话。

- **vicious**
  ['vɪʃəs]
  ⓐ 邪恶的、凶残的

  i can't believe my neighbor is actually a vicious man.
  我不敢相信我的邻居实际上是个邪恶的人。

- **wicked**
  ['wɪkɪd]
  ⓐ 邪恶的

  The wicked witch was riding a broomstick.
  邪恶的女巫正骑着扫帚。

- **evil**
  ['ivl]
  ⓐ 邪恶的

  He really put his evil thoughts into practice.
  他真的将他邪恶的想法付诸实施。

- **infamous**
  ['ɪnfəməs]
  ⓐ 声名狼藉的

  He was infamous for his anti-feminist attitude.
  他因反对女权主义的态度而声名狼藉。

- **sinful**
  ['sɪnfl]
  ⓐ 不道德的、有罪的

  In some cultures, adultery is regarded as sinful.
  在一些文化中,通奸被视为不道德的。

- **dishonest**
  [dɪs'ɑnɪst]
  ⓐ 不诚实的

  Dishonest behavior won't be tolerated in our company.
  我们公司不容许不诚实的行为。　→ tolerate 表示"容忍"

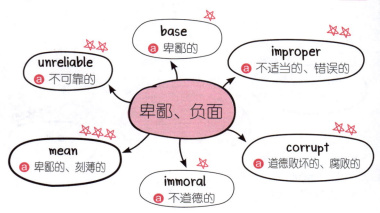

- **base**
  [beɪs]
  ⓐ 卑鄙的

  Do you have any base idea in your mind?
  你心中有没有任何卑鄙的念头？

- **improper**
  [ɪmˈprɑːpər]
  ⓐ 不适当的、错误的

  It's improper to lie to your beloved ones.
  欺骗自己所爱的人是不对的。

- **corrupt**
  [kəˈrʌpt]
  ⓐ 道德败坏的、腐败的

  This is a corrupt society. Most people are greedy and selfish.
  这是一个道德败坏的社会，大部分的人贪婪又自私。
  → greedy 表示"贪婪的"

- **immoral**
  [ɪˈmɔːrəl]
  ⓐ 不道德的

  Reading other people's diaries is immoral.
  偷看别人的日记是不道德的。

- **mean**
  [miːn]
  ⓐ 卑鄙的、刻薄的

  You are my best friend. Why are you so mean to me?
  你是我最好的朋友，为什么你对我这么刻薄？

- **unreliable**
  [ˌʌnrɪˈlaɪəbl]
  ⓐ 不可靠的

  I don't trust him. He is a liar and he is unreliable.
  我不信任他，他是一个骗子，而且不可靠。

# Lesson 11

# follow
['faloʊ]

## 跟随我,你会了解我

**follow** 动词表示"跟随、接着、理解、采用"。

- A strange man has been following me for a while.
  一个陌生男子已跟随我一阵子了。　→ for a while 表示"一会儿"

- Don't tell me what to do. I don't want to follow your advice.
  不要告诉我做什么,我不想听你的建议。

- Please slow down. I don't quite follow you.
  请讲慢一点儿,我不太明白你在说什么。

- Please make sure you follow the instructions, otherwise you might make a mistake.
  请务必依照指示做,不然你有可能会做错。

- New students should follow the staff with a red flag; they will show you around the campus.
  新生请跟着拿着红色旗子的工作人员,他们会带你们参观校园。

**美国人常用短语**

- **for a while** 一会儿
- **comply with** 遵守
- **under the misapprehension** 误以为

（相关词汇群组记忆）

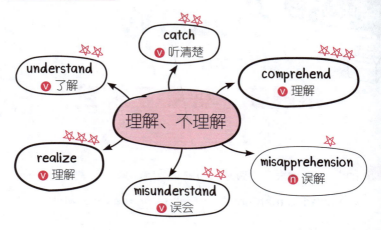

- **catch**
  [kætʃ]
  **v** 听清楚

  Sorry, I didn't catch your name.
  抱歉，我没听清楚你的名字。

- **comprehend**
  [ˌkɑmprɪ'hend]
  **v** 理解

  Ryan totally doesn't comprehend how his car bumped into a tree.
  莱恩完全不理解他的车是怎么撞上树的。

- **misapprehension**
  [ˌmɪsæprɪ'henʃn]
  **n** 误解

  I was under the misapprehension that he was divorced.
  我误以为他已经离婚了。
  → under the misapprehension 表示"误以为"

- **misunderstand**
  [ˌmɪsʌndər'stænd]
  **v** 误会

  I misunderstood you. I must offer you an apology.
  我误会你了。我必须向你道歉。

- **realize**
  ['rɪəlaɪz]
  **v** 理解

  Don't you realize how serious this accident was?
  你难道不了解这个事故有多严重吗？

- **understand**
  [ˌʌndər'stænd]
  **v** 了解

  I don't understand why he did this to me.
  我不了解为什么他对我这么做。

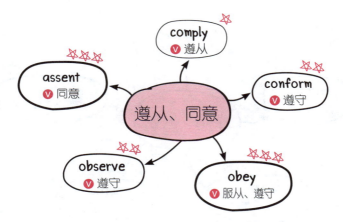

- **comply**
  [kəm'plaɪ]
  **v** 遵从

  You have to comply with the rules of the game.
  你必须遵守比赛规则。 → comply with 表示"遵守"

- **conform**
  [kən'fɔrm]
  **v** 遵守

  Everyone should conform to the traffic rules.
  每个人都应该遵守交通规则。 → conform to 表示"遵守"

- **obey**
  [ə'beɪ]
  **v** 服从、遵守

  If you fail to obey the law, you will be punished.
  如果你没有遵守法律，你就会被处罚。

- **observe**
  [əb'zɜrv]
  **v** 遵守

  Austin and Vivian observed the traditional wedding customs.
  奥斯汀与薇薇安遵守传统婚姻习俗。

- **assent**
  [ə'sent]
  **v** 同意

  We assented to adopt the new policy.
  我们同意采用新政策。

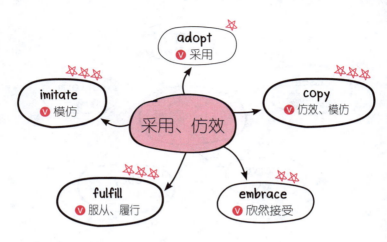

- **adopt**
  [əˈdɑpt]
  Ⓥ 采用

  This factory will adopt a new drainage system.
  这家工厂将采用新的排水系统。

- **copy**
  [ˈkɑpi]
  Ⓥ 仿效、模仿

  You have to be creative. Don't copy others' ideas.
  你要有创意，不要模仿别人的点子。

- **embrace**
  [ɪmˈbreɪs]
  Ⓥ 欣然接受

  All the team members embraced the new diet plan.
  所有团队成员都欣然接受新的饮食计划。

- **fulfill**
  [fʊlˈfɪl]
  Ⓥ 服从、履行

  The police should always fulfill their duty of protecting the citizens.
  警方应该永远尽责保护市民。　→ duty 表示"责任"

- **imitate**
  [ˈɪmɪteɪt]
  Ⓥ 模仿

  My five-year-old son was imitating my laughter.
  我五岁的儿子在模仿我的笑声。

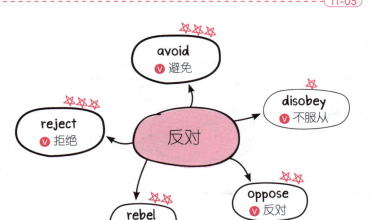

- **avoid**
  [ə'vɔɪd]
  v 避免

  He avoids making the same mistakes.
  他避免犯同样的错误。

- **disobey**
  [ˌdɪsə'beɪ]
  v 不服从

  Zack was expelled from school for disobeying the school regulations.
  查克由于不服从校规而被学校开除。

  → expel 表示"开除"也可以用下列短语来表示：
  be dismissed from school / flunk out of school

- **oppose**
  [ə'poʊz]
  v 反对

  Why do you always oppose the government's policies?
  你为什么总是反对政府的政策？

- **rebel**
  [rɪ'bɛl]
  v 反抗

  Most teenagers rebel against their parents to prove their independence.
  大部分青少年会反抗他们的父母，以证明他们的独立。

- **reject**
  [rɪ'dʒɛkt]
  v 拒绝

  Norman's parole application was rejected again.
  诺曼的假释申请又被拒绝了。 → parole 表示"假释"

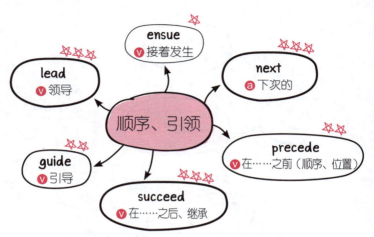

- **ensue**
  [ɪnˈsu]
  v 接着发生

  The war was finally over and peace ensued.
  战争终于结束,和平随之到来。

- **next**
  [nekst]
  a 下次的

  When will the next assembly take place?
  何时举行下次集会? → assembly 表示"集会"

- **precede**
  [prɪˈsid]
  v 在……之前(顺序、位置)

  Usually an engagement party precedes a wedding ceremony.
  订婚宴通常在结婚典礼之前。

- **succeed**
  [səkˈsid]
  v 在……之后、继承

  The prince succeeded to the throne after his father passed away.
  王子在他父亲过世后继承王位。

- **guide**
  [gaɪd]
  v 引导

  My father helped me and guided me through the hard time I had.
  我父亲帮助我并引导我度过艰难的时刻。

- **lead**
  [lid]
  v 领导

  The king will lead the army to fight.
  国王将领导军队打仗。

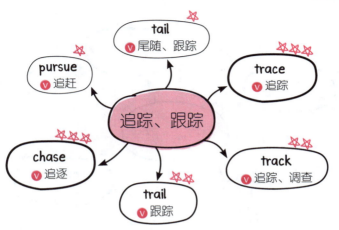

- **tail**
  [teɪl]
  v 尾随、跟踪

  A man in a black coat was tailing me.
  一名穿黑色大衣的男子尾随着我。

- **trace**
  [treɪs]
  v 追踪

  They traced footprints in the forest.
  他们追踪森林里的脚印。

- **track**
  [træk]
  v 追踪、调查

  The police were tracking a vehicle.
  警方正在跟踪一辆车。

- **trail**
  [treɪl]
  v 跟踪

  A hunter was trailing a deer.
  猎人正在跟踪一头鹿。

- **chase**
  [tʃeɪs]
  v 追逐

  Those kids are chasing butterflies.
  那些小孩正在追逐蝴蝶。

- **pursue**
  [pərˈsu]
  v 追赶

  I saw a cat pursuing a rat.
  我看到一只猫正在追老鼠。

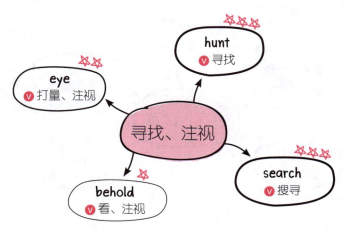

▶ **hunt**
[hʌnt]
ⓥ 寻找

I've been busy **hunting** jobs.
我一直忙着找工作。

▶ **search**
[sɜrtʃ]
ⓥ 搜寻

They kept **searching** for survivors from this shipwreck.
他们继续搜寻这场船难的生还者。

▶ **behold**
[bɪˈhoʊld]
ⓥ 看、注视

Niagara Falls is such a spectacular scene to **behold**.
尼亚加拉瀑布看起来真是壮观。
→ spectacular 表示 "壮观的"

▶ **eye**
[aɪ]
ⓥ 打量、注视

The way he **eyes** me makes me nervous.
他看我的样子令我紧张。

# Lesson 12

# improve
[ɪm'pruv]

### 事情一定有所改善

💬 **improve** 动词表示 "改善、提升"。

- My math test score improved after a lot of practice.
  经过多次练习,我的数学测验分数提高了。

- This restaurant improved their service and food quality.
  这家餐厅改善了他们的服务与食物品质。

- Veronica learned to dance to improve her poise.
  薇若妮卡学习跳舞以提升平衡感。 → poise 表示 "平衡"

- You can go to a cram school to improve your English ability.
  你可以去补习班提升你的英语能力。

- The best way to improve your skill is to practice a lot.
  提升技能的最佳方法是勤加练习。

**美国人常用短语**

- **in vain** 徒劳的
- **give up** 放弃
- **a series of** 一连串的
- **face up to** 勇敢地面对
- **you have my word** 我向你保证

（相关词汇群组记忆）

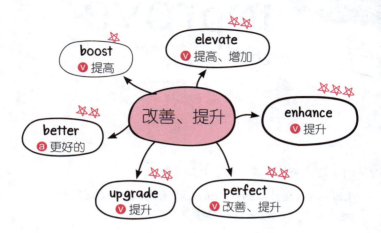

- **elevate**
  ['elɪveɪt]
  v 提高、增加

  Consuming too much sugar can elevate your blood sugar level.
  吃进太多糖分会使你的血糖升高。 → consume 表示"吃、喝"

- **enhance**
  [ɪn'hæns]
  v 提升

  How can I enhance my English proficiency?
  我要如何提升我的英语水平？

- **perfect**
  ['pɜrfɪkt]
  v 改善、提升

  The main purpose of this seminar is to enhance and perfect the social skills.
  此次研讨会的主要目的是提升与改善社交技巧。

- **upgrade**
  ['ʌpgreɪd]
  v 提升

  I upgraded my smart phone because my old one was getting too slow.
  我把我的智能手机升级了，因为旧的太慢了。

- **better**
  ['betər]
  a 更好的

  Visual effects of 3D movies are better than before.
  三维电影的视觉效果比以前更好。

- **boost**
  [bust]
  v 提高

  The childbirth subsidy policy is expected to boost the birth rate.
  生育补助政策促进生育率。

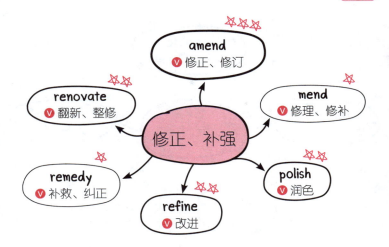

- **amend**
  [əˈmɛnd]
  V 修正、修订

  *The Copyright Act* was amended in March.
  《著作权法》于三月进行了修订。  → Act（大写）表示"法案"

- **mend**
  [mɛnd]
  V 修理、修补

  It took me the whole afternoon to mend the toilet.
  我花了一整个下午修理马桶。

- **polish**
  [ˈpɑlɪʃ]
  V 润色

  This article needs to be polished.
  这篇文章需要润色。

- **refine**
  [rɪˈfaɪn]
  V 改进

  Food processing has been refined.
  食品加工过程不断改进。

- **remedy**
  [ˈrɛmədɪ]
  V 补救、纠正

  They tried so hard to remedy the problem but it was in vain.
  他们非常努力地补救问题，但是这是徒劳的。
  → in vain 表示"徒劳的"

- **renovate**
  [ˈrɛnəvet]
  V 翻新、整修

  This haunted castle was renovated many times.
  这座闹鬼的城堡翻新过多次。

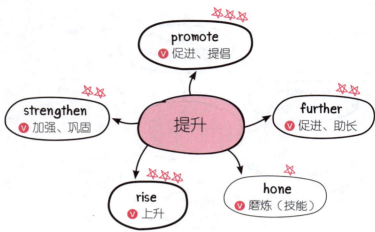

- **promote**
  [prə'mout]
  Ⓥ 促进、提倡

  Some religious groups try to promote the idea of vegetarianism.
  有些宗教团体试着提倡素食的概念。
  → vegetarianism 表示 "素食主义"

- **further**
  ['fɜrðər]
  Ⓥ 促进、助长

  You can further your knowledge through reading.
  你可以通过阅读增进知识。

- **hone**
  [houn]
  Ⓥ 磨炼（技能）

  I haven't honed my tennis skills for many years.
  我许多年没有练习我的网球技巧了。

- **rise**
  [raɪz]
  Ⓥ 上升

  The number of foreign tourists visiting China has been rising.
  到中国旅游的外国游客人数不断上升。

- **strengthen**
  ['strɛŋθn]
  Ⓥ 加强、巩固

  I will strengthen my will and never give up.
  我会加强我的意志并且绝不放弃。  → give up 表示 "放弃"

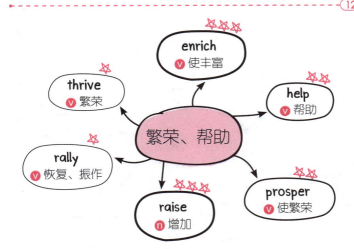

- **enrich**
 [ɪnˈrɪtʃ]
 v 使丰富

 Studying abroad is an opportunity to enrich your life.
 出国留学是使你的人生更丰富的一个机会。

- **help**
 [hɛlp]
 v 帮助

 Can you help me remove this desk?
 你能不能帮我移开这张桌子？

- **prosper**
 [ˈprɑspər]
 v 使繁荣

 The company has been prospering greatly since George took it over.
 公司自从乔治接手之后，就一直非常成功。

- **raise**
 [reɪz]
 n 增加

 It's hard to get a pay raise.
 加薪并不容易。

- **rally**
 [ˈræli]
 v 恢复、振作

 After a weekend's rest, I rallied a little.
 经过一个周末的休息，我身体复原了一些。

- **thrive**
 [θraɪv]
 v 繁荣

 Cultural exchange between China and South Korea have started to thrive in recent years.
 中国与韩国之间的文化交流近些年来开始兴盛。

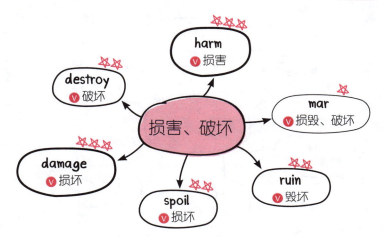

- **harm**
  [hɑrm]
  Ⓥ 损害

  Drinking too much wine will harm your health.
  喝太多的葡萄酒会损害你的健康。

- **mar**
  [mɑr]
  Ⓥ 损毁、破坏

  Our vacation was marred by a series of incidents.
  我们的假期被一连串事件给毁了。　→ a series of 表示"一连串的"

- **ruin**
  ['ruɪn]
  Ⓥ 毁坏

  You just ruined my dress. It's very expensive.
  你毁坏了我的连衣裙，这很贵。

- **spoil**
  [spɔɪl]
  Ⓥ 损坏

  The noise from the drilling from outside really spoiled my mood.
  外面传来的钻孔噪声真是破坏我的心情。　→ drilling 表示"钻孔"

- **damage**
  ['dæmɪdʒ]
  Ⓥ 损坏

  These young men damaged cars in the parking lot on purpose.
  这些年轻人故意损毁停车场里的车。

- **destroy**
  [dɪ'strɔɪ]
  Ⓥ 破坏

  You completely destroyed my five-year-old daughter's imagination about fairy tales.
  你彻底毁了我五岁女儿对童话的幻想。

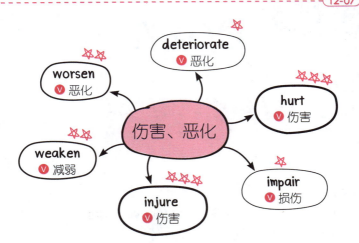

- **deteriorate**
  [dɪˈtɪrɪəreɪt]
  Ⓥ 恶化

  Her condition deteriorated substantially in a few days.
  她的病情在几天内大幅恶化。
  → substantially 表示 "大量地"

- **hurt**
  [hɜrt]
  Ⓥ 伤害

  I will never hurt you. You have my word.
  我绝不会伤害你，我向你保证。
  → you have my word 表示 "我向你保证"

- **impair**
  [ɪmˈper]
  Ⓥ 损伤

  The explosion impaired his hearing.
  爆炸使他的听力受损。

- **injure**
  [ˈɪndʒər]
  Ⓥ 伤害

  Johnny's knee was injured after he slipped in the bathroom.
  强尼在浴室滑倒后膝盖受伤了。

- **weaken**
  [ˈwikən]
  Ⓥ 减弱

  Nothing can weaken my confidence in myself.
  没有什么能够减弱我的自信。

- **worsen**
  [ˈwɜrsn]
  Ⓥ 恶化

  You have to face up to the truth that her cancer was worsening.
  你必须勇敢面对她癌症恶化的事实。
  → face up to 表示 "勇敢地面对"

# Lesson 13 learn

[lɜrn]

## 有好多事情要学习

💬 **learn** 动词表示"学习、得知、认识到、记住"。

- I've been **learning** German for five years.
  我学德语已经五年了。

- We **learned** that he died of lung cancer last month.
  我们得知他上个月死于肺癌。 → die of... 表示"死于……"

- From this experience she **learned** that failure is part of the process leading to success.
  从这个经验,她学到失败是迈向成功的部分过程。 → lead to 表示"通往"

- What did you **learn** in school today?
  你今天在学校学了什么呢?

- I have been wanting to **learn** how to play the piano since I was 10 years old.
  我从十岁开始就一直想要学钢琴。

**美国人常用短语**

- **lead to** 通往
- **stay up** 熬夜
- **dig up** 发现
- **turn in** 上交、归还
- **figure out** 理解
- **find out** 查明

相关词汇群组记忆

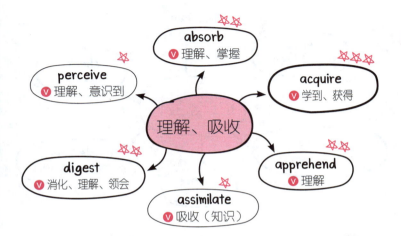

- **absorb**
  [əb'zɔrb]
  v 理解、掌握

  We can absorb a lot of information quickly through the media.
  我们可通过媒体快速掌握许多信息。

- **acquire**
  [ə'kwaɪər]
  v 学到、获得

  He acquired carving skills from the sculpture class.
  他从雕刻课学到雕刻技巧。

- **apprehend**
  [ˌæprɪ'hend]
  v 理解

  I don't apprehend why you don't like me.
  我无法理解为什么你不喜欢我。

- **assimilate**
  [ə'sɪməleɪt]
  v 吸收（知识）

  I try to assimilate as much knowledge as I can.
  我尝试吸收尽可能多的知识。

- **digest**
  [daɪ'dʒest]
  v 消化、理解、领会

  I don't have enough time to digest so much information.
  我没有足够的时间来消化这么多信息。

- **perceive**
  [pər'siv]
  v 理解、意识到

  I gradually perceived that she was not what she appeared to be.
  我逐渐了解到她是个表里不一的人。

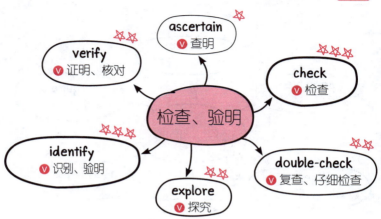

- **ascertain**
  [ˌæsərˈteɪn]
  v 查明

  The investigation was ongoing to ascertain what caused the fire.
  调查持续进行，以便查出火灾的原因。
  → ongoing 表示"进行的"

- **check**
  [tʃek]
  v 检查

  I called the gas company to check out the gas pipe.
  我打电话叫燃气公司来检查燃气管道。

- **double-check**
  [ˈdʌbl tʃek]
  v 复查、仔细检查

  Be sure to double-check the answer before turning in the exam paper.
  交考卷之前务必复查答案。 → turn in 表示"上交、归还"

- **explore**
  [ɪkˈsplɔr]
  v 探究

  The main theme of this article is to explore the law of attraction.
  本文的主题是要探究吸引力法则。

- **identify**
  [aɪˈdentɪfaɪ]
  v 识别、验明

  My father can identify birds by their sounds.
  我父亲可以靠声音识别鸟类。

- **verify**
  [ˈverɪfaɪ]
  v 证明、核对

  I tried to verify whether he told the truth or not.
  我设法证明他是否说的是真话。

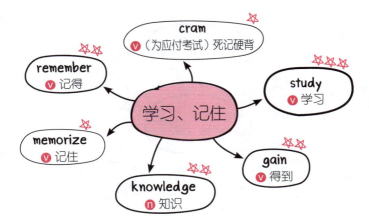

- **cram**
  [kræm]
  v（为应付考试）死记硬背

  Last night, I stayed up late and crammed for today's test.
  为了今天的考试,昨天晚上我熬夜死记硬背。
  → stay up 表示"熬夜"

- **study**
  ['stʌdi]
  v 学习

  He was studying English for the test next week.
  他为了下周的测验而念英语。

- **gain**
  [geɪn]
  v 得到

  He worked hard to gain all kinds of knowledge.
  他非常努力要获得所有种类的知识。

- **knowledge**
  ['nɑlɪdʒ]
  n 知识

  Knowledge and wisdom are different.
  知识与智慧是不同的。

- **memorize**
  ['meməraɪz]
  v 记住

  He memorized every word I said.
  他记得我说的每句话。

- **remember**
  [rɪ'membər]
  v 记得

  She remembered every line from this movie.
  她记得这部电影的所有台词。

- **discover**
  [dɪˈskʌvər]
  v 发现

  I discovered that he was a hypocrite.
  我发现他是个伪君子。 → hypocrite 表示"伪君子"

- **find**
  [faɪnd]
  v 发现

  Tim wanted to find out who framed him.
  蒂姆想要查出是谁陷害他的。

- **sense**
  [sens]
  v 感觉到、意识到

  Benjamin sensed that something was wrong here.
  本杰明感觉到这里有点儿不太对劲。

- **uncover**
  [ʌnˈkʌvər]
  v 揭露

  The journalist uncovered this conspiracy.
  记者揭露了此项阴谋。 → conspiracy 表示"阴谋"

- **dig**
  [dɪg]
  v 挖掘

  Our team tried to dig up the mystery of near-death experiences.
  我们的团队试图找出濒死经验之谜。 → dig up 表示"发现"

- **detect**
  [dɪˈtekt]
  v 察觉、发现

  Diabetes is hard to detect in the early stage.
  糖尿病在初期很难察觉。 → diabetes 表示"糖尿病"

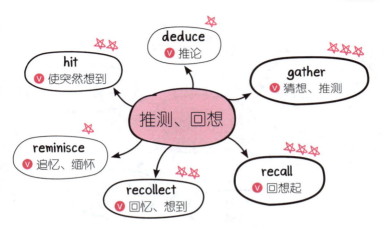

- **deduce**
  [dɪˈdus]
  v 推论

  There was not enough evidence to deduce Nick stole the money.
  没有足够证据可推论尼克偷了钱。

- **gather**
  [ˈgæðər]
  v 猜想、推测

  I gathered that you wanted to apologize to me.
  我猜你想要向我道歉。

- **recall**
  [rɪˈkɔl]
  v 回想起

  I recalled that I fell asleep when I saw the musical Les Misérables on Broadway.
  我想起我在百老汇看音乐剧《悲惨世界》时睡着了。

- **recollect**
  [ˌrekəˈlekt]
  v 回忆、想到

  I don't recollect why he broke up with me.
  我想不起来他为什么和我分手。

- **reminisce**
  [ˌreməˈnɪs]
  v 追忆、缅怀

  Wilson likes to reminisce about his years in the service.
  威尔森喜欢回忆从军那几年的日子。

- **hit**
  [hɪt]
  v 使突然想到

  It hits me that today was our tenth wedding anniversary.
  我突然想到今天是我们结婚十周年的纪念日。
  → anniversary 表示"周年纪念日"

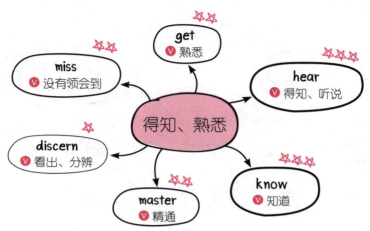

- **get**
  [gɛt]
  Ⓥ 熟悉

  It took me a while to get into the company.
  我花了一段时间才熟悉新公司。 → get into 表示"熟悉"

- **hear**
  [hɪr]
  Ⓥ 得知、听说

  I heard that she was back from London yesterday.
  我听说她昨天从伦敦回来了。

- **know**
  [noʊ]
  Ⓥ 知道

  I know how to make a perfect omelet.
  我知道怎么做出完美的煎蛋卷。 → omelet 表示"煎蛋卷"

- **master**
  ['mæstər]
  Ⓥ 精通

  How long will it take to master a language?
  要精通一种语言需要多长时间?

- **discern**
  [dɪ'sɜrn]
  Ⓥ 看出、分辨

  It's hard to discern his intention.
  很难看出他的意图。 → intention 表示"意图、目的"

- **miss**
  [mɪs]
  Ⓥ 没有领会到

  I'm sorry I missed your point.
  抱歉我不明白你的意思。

# look

[lʊk]

## 外表看起来怎么样

14-01

**Part 2** 美国人最常用的单词

💬 **look** 动词表示"看、看起来、注意"；
名词表示"看、外表、表情"。

- He smiled with a sad **look**.
  他微笑着，但表情悲伤。

- She is forty years old but still **looks** like a teenager.
  她四十岁了，但看起来仍像个少女。

- Take a **look** at these amazing photos taken at the Atlantic Ocean Road.
  看看这些在大西洋海滨公路所拍的精彩照片。 → take a look at 表示"看一看"

- **Look**! There's a little cat under the car.
  你看！有一只小猫在车底下。

【美国人常用短语】

- **take a look at** 看一看
- **break up** 分手
- **on pins and needles** 坐立不安
- **in good shape** 身体健康
- **gaze at** 凝视
- **glare at** 怒视
- **peek at** 偷看
- **peer at** 凝视
- **spy on** 暗中监视
- **stare at** 盯着看
- **had better...** 最好……

## 相关词汇群组记忆

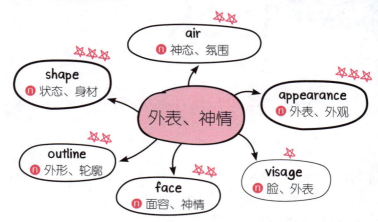

- **air** [er]
  n 神态、氛围、

  There is a mysterious air about the Moai statues on Easter Island.
  复活节岛上的摩艾石像有一种神秘的氛围。
  → statue 表示"雕像"

- **appearance** [əˈpɪrəns]
  n 外表、外观

  The appearance of this area looked worn and dirty.
  这个区域的外观看起来破旧且脏乱。

- **visage** [ˈvɪzɪdʒ]
  n 脸、外表

  She has a delicate visage.
  她有一张精致的脸孔。 → delicate 表示"精致的、精美的"

- **face** [feɪs]
  n 面容、神情

  When he walked in, his face looked serious.
  当他走进来时，表情看起来很严肃。

- **outline** [ˈaʊtlaɪn]
  n 外形、轮廓

  My four-year-old daughter is drawing the outline of a car.
  我四岁的女儿正在画一辆车的轮廓。

- **shape** [ʃeɪp]
  n 状态、身材

  He is ninety years old, but he is still in good shape.
  他九十岁了，但是身体仍然很健康。

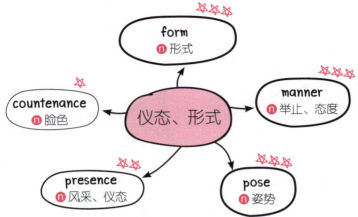

▶ **form**
[fɔːrm]
ⓝ 形式

Abstract art is a unique form of art.
抽象艺术是一种独特的艺术形式。

▶ **manner**
[ˈmænər]
ⓝ 举止、态度

Students should have a respectful manner to teachers.
学生应该以尊敬的态度对待老师。

▶ **pose**
[poʊz]
ⓝ 姿势

Today we're going to learn some basic yoga poses.
今天我们要学习瑜伽的一些基本姿势。

▶ **presence**
[ˈprezns]
ⓝ 风采、仪态

She is an elegant woman with a charming presence.
她是个仪态优雅且迷人的女人。

▶ **countenance**
[ˈkaʊntənəns]
ⓝ 脸色

She is skinny and of a pale countenance.
她骨瘦如柴且脸色苍白。 → pale 表示"苍白的"

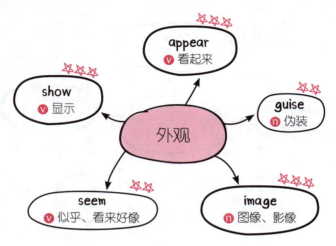

▶ **appear**
[ə'pɪr]
Ⓥ 看起来

It **appeared** that he broke up with his girlfriend.
看来他跟他女朋友分手了。 → break up 表示"分手"

▶ **guise**
[gaɪz]
Ⓝ 伪装

I went to the costume party in the **guise** of a vampire.
我装扮成吸血鬼的样子去化装舞会。

▶ **image**
['ɪmɪdʒ]
Ⓝ 图像、影像

I took a picture of the reflected **image** in the lake.
我照了一张湖中倒影的照片。

▶ **seem**
[sim]
Ⓥ 似乎、看来好像

Megan **seemed** to be on pins and needles.
梅根看来好像坐立不安。
→ on pins and needles 表示"坐立不安"

▶ **show**
[ʃoʊ]
Ⓥ 显示

She **showed** her gratitude to me.
她向我表达感激。

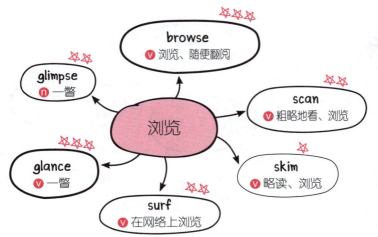

- **browse**
  [braʊz]
  v 浏览、随便翻阅

  I was browsing the newspaper while having a cup of coffee.
  我边喝咖啡，边浏览报纸。

- **scan**
  [skæn]
  v 粗略地看、浏览

  I scanned the menu quickly and decided what I wanted to order.
  我快速浏览菜单，并决定好我要点什么。

- **skim**
  [skɪm]
  v 略读、浏览

  I skimmed through this article and found it very interesting.
  我大概读了这篇文章，发现文章很有趣。

- **surf**
  [sɜrf]
  v 在网络上浏览

  Many people spend the whole day surfing the Internet.
  很多人花一整天时间上网。

- **glance**
  [glæns]
  v 一瞥

  I was glancing through today's newspaper.
  我正在浏览今天的报纸。

- **glimpse**
  [glɪmps]
  n 一瞥

  I had a glimpse of his eyes.
  我瞥见他的眼神。

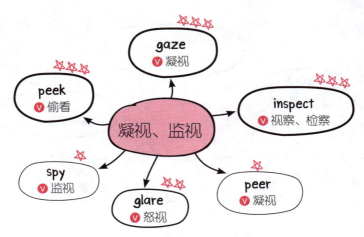

- **gaze**
[geɪz]
v 凝视

  That man kept gazing at me like I was an acquaintance.
  那个人一直凝视着我,好像我是熟人一样。
  → gaze at 表示"凝视"

- **inspect**
[ɪn'spekt]
v 视察、检察

  The firefighters inspected the house after the fire.
  火灾后,消防员去检查房屋。

- **peer**
[pɪr]
v 凝视

  We are peering at the train schedule.
  我们盯着火车时刻表看。 → peer at 表示"凝视"

- **glare**
[gler]
v 怒视

  They are glaring at each other angrily.
  他们正生气地怒目相对。 → glare at 表示"怒视"

- **spy**
[spaɪ]
v 监视

  The government has been spying on him for many years.
  政府已经暗中监视他好几年了。 → spy on 表示"暗中监视"

- **peek**
[pik]
v 偷看

  I was peeking at him through the window.
  我从窗户偷看他。 → peek at 表示"偷看"

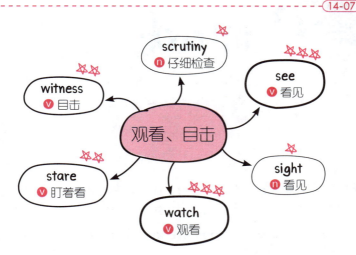

- **scrutiny**
  ['skrutəni]
  **n** 仔细检查

  This contract was under scrutiny.
  这份合约经过了仔细的检查。

- **see**
  [si]
  **v** 看见

  I saw some kids flying a kite in the park.
  我看到一些小孩在公园放风筝。

- **sight**
  [saɪt]
  **n** 看见

  I don't believe in love at first sight.
  我不相信一见钟情。

- **watch**
  [watʃ]
  **v** 观看

  You had better not watch TV for a long time.
  你最好不要看电视看太久。　→ had better 表示"最好"

- **stare**
  [ster]
  **v** 盯着看

  A stranger in the corner was staring at me.
  角落的一位陌生人正在盯着我看。　→ stare at 表示"盯着看"

- **witness**
  ['wɪtnəs]
  **v** 目击

  I just witnessed a shooting star.
  我刚刚看到流星了。

## Lesson 15

# mind

[maɪnd]

## 我的心里非常介意

💬 **mind** 动词表示"介意、反对、注意、专心于";
名词表示"头脑、智力、想法、理性"。

- Bear in mind that you have to be careful when you walk alone in the dark.
  要记住当你一个人走在暗处时千万要小心。 → bear in mind 表示"记住"

- Do you mind if I put my socks on the sofa?
  你介意我把我的袜子放在沙发上吗?

- Mind your step when you go down the stairs.
  下楼时留意你的脚步。

- Would you mind changing seats with me?
  你介意和我换个位置吗?

- I don't mind you sitting next to me, but can you try not to talk with your mouth full?
  我不介意你坐在我的旁边,但你可不可以吃东西的时候不要讲话?

### 美国人常用短语

- **bear in mind** 记住
- **pay attention to** 注意
- **disapprove of...** 不赞成……
- **suffer from** 受(某种病痛)折磨

相关词汇群组记忆

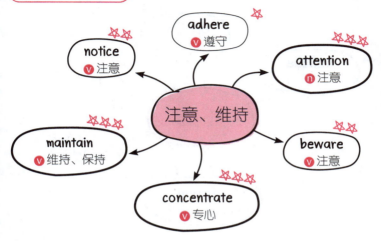

▶**adhere**
[əd'hɪr]
ⓥ 遵守

Some people are unable to adhere to the social norms.
有些人不遵守社会规范。

▶**attention**
[ə'tenʃn]
ⓝ 注意

He never paid attention to his children.
他从不注意他的小孩。 → pay attention to 表示"注意"

▶**beware**
[bɪ'wer]
ⓥ 注意

Beware of the calories you intake if you want to lose weight.
如果你想要减重,就要注意卡路里的摄取。

▶**concentrate**
['kɑnsntreɪt]
ⓥ 专心

Turn down the music. I need to concentrate on my studies now.
音乐关小声一点。我现在需要专心读书。
→ turn down 表示"关小"

▶**maintain**
[meɪn'teɪn]
ⓥ 维持、保持

We should develop and maintain a positive attitude towards everything.
我们对所有事情应该培养并保持正面的态度。

▶**notice**
['noʊtɪs]
ⓥ 注意

I didn't notice that you changed your hairstyle.
我没注意到你改变发型了。

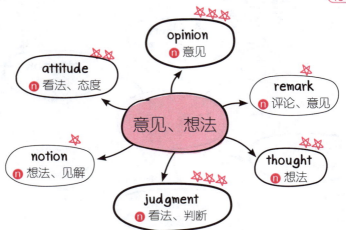

- **opinion**
  [ə'pɪnjən]
  n 意见

  In my opinion, the current economic policy has an adverse impact on the country's economic development.
  依我来看，目前的经济政策对于国家经济发展有不利影响。

- **remark**
  [rɪ'mɑrk]
  n 评论、意见

  Dr. Lee made a remark about the impact of technology on the environment.
  李博士就科技对环境的影响提出意见。

- **thought**
  [θɔt]
  n 想法

  You never reveal your thoughts to me.
  你从不对我透露你的想法。

- **judgment**
  ['dʒʌdʒmənt]
  n 看法、判断

  Max is a mentor to me. I can always count on his judgment.
  麦克斯是我的精神导师，我总是依赖于他的判断。

- **notion**
  ['noʊʃn]
  n 想法、见解

  We have very different notions about education.
  我们对教育的见解是非常不同的。

- **attitude**
  ['ætɪtud]
  n 看法、态度

  My attitude toward reincarnation is different from yours.
  我对转世的看法与你的不同。　→ reincarnation 表示"转世"

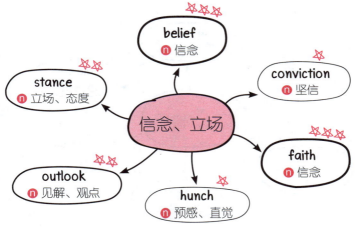

- **belief**
  [bɪ'liːf]
  n 信念

  As a teacher I embrace the belief that every student is unique and equally important.
  作为一名老师，我怀抱的信念是每个学生都是独特的，并且同等重要。

- **conviction**
  [kən'vɪkʃn]
  n 坚信

  Jamie has a strong conviction that every woman is made from a man's rib.
  杰米坚信每个女人都是从男人的一根肋骨变来的。

- **faith**
  [feɪθ]
  n 信念

  I always have the faith that I will achieve my goals.
  我总是保持信念，相信我将达成目标。

- **hunch**
  [hʌntʃ]
  n 预感、直觉

  Stephan has a hunch that he's going to hit the jackpot this time.
  史蒂芬有预感他这次会中大奖。

- **outlook**
  ['aʊtlʊk]
  n 见解、观点

  I've been through a culture shock and it changed my outlook on many things thoroughly.
  我经历过文化冲击，这彻底改变了我对很多事的看法。

- **stance**
  [stæns]
  n 立场、态度

  What's your stance on the development of nuclear energy?
  你对核能发展的立场是什么？

115

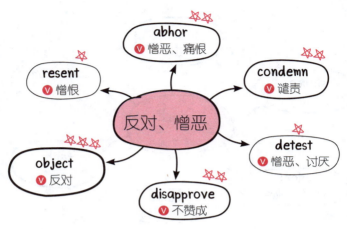

> **abhor**
> [əbˈhɔr]
> ⓥ 憎恶、痛恨

Most people abhor cyberbullying, which caused many social problems.
大部分的人都痛恨网络欺凌，其已造成许多社会问题。

> **condemn**
> [kənˈdem]
> ⓥ 谴责

The cyclist was condemned for using drugs.
这名自行车手由于使用禁药而被谴责。

> **detest**
> [dɪˈtest]
> ⓥ 憎恶、讨厌

Harry's wife detests cooking and cleaning.
哈利的妻子讨厌煮饭与打扫工作。

> **disapprove**
> [ˌdɪsəˈpruv]
> ⓥ 不赞成

Some people disapproved of the way the president dealt with the problem of racial discrimination.
有些人不赞成总统处理种族歧视问题的方式。

> **object**
> [ˈabdʒekt]
> ⓥ 反对

All the staff object to the alternative plan.
所有职员都反对替代方案。

> **resent**
> [rɪˈzent]
> ⓥ 憎恨

I resent your domineering attitude towards me.
你对我跋扈的态度令我厌恶。　→ domineering 表示"跋扈的"

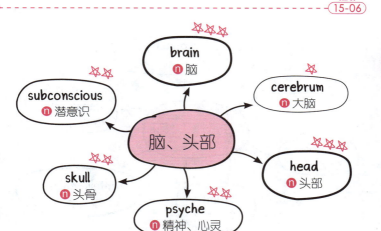

▶ **brain**
[breɪn]
n 脑

She has been suffering from brain injury since the car accident.
自从车祸后,她就遭受到脑损伤的折磨。
→ suffer from 表示"受(某种疼痛)折磨"

▶ **cerebrum**
[səˈribrəm]
n 大脑

The cerebrum is responsible for many cognitive functions.
大脑负责许多认知功能。

▶ **head**
[hed]
n 头部

My head was aching when I woke up this morning.
我今天早上醒来时头很痛。 → ache 表示"疼痛"

▶ **psyche**
[ˈsaɪki]
n 精神、心灵

There are so many interesting things to explore about the human psyche.
关于人类的心灵,有许多有趣的事物可探索。

▶ **skull**
[skʌl]
n 头骨

Jeff's dog dug up a skull from the neighbor's garden.
杰夫的狗从邻居的花园中挖出一个头骨。

▶ **subconscious**
[ˌsʌbˈkɑnʃəs]
n 潜意识

The subject of my thesis is about the subconscious mind.
我的论文主题与潜意识有关。 → thesis 表示"论文"

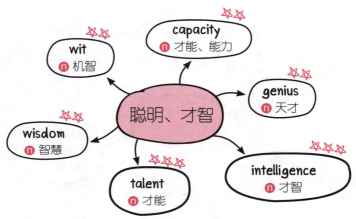

- **capacity**
  [kəˈpæsəti]
  n 才能、能力

  I was impressed by her capacity for leadership.
  我很佩服她的领导能力。　→ impress 表示"使钦佩"

- **genius**
  [ˈdʒiniəs]
  n 天才

  How do you come up with so many brilliant ideas? You are such a genius.
  你是怎么想出这么多如此棒的点子的？你真是个天才。
  → come up with 表示"想出"

- **intelligence**
  [ɪnˈtelɪdʒəns]
  n 才智

  She took a high score in the intelligence test.
  她在智力测验中得到了高分。

- **talent**
  [ˈtælənt]
  n 才能

  Students should develop diverse talents and interests as much as possible.
  学生应尽可能培养多样化的才能与兴趣。

- **wisdom**
  [ˈwɪzdəm]
  n 智慧

  We need wisdom to cope with challenges in life.
  我们需要智慧来应付人生的挑战。　→ cope with 表示"解决"

- **wit**
  [wɪt]
  n 机智

  Cindy used her wit to break the ice.
  辛迪用她的机智来化解尴尬。　→ break the ice 表示"打破僵局"

## Lesson 16

# problem

['prɑbləm]

## 问题好多，困难重重

**problem** 名词表示"问题、麻烦"。

- His rashness brought about so many **problems**.
  他的鲁莽造成了许多麻烦。　→ bring about 表示"引起"

- Did you have any solution to the **problem**?
  你有没有问题的解决方案？

- I have serious allergic **problems**.
  我有严重的过敏问题。

- What is your **problem**? Stop talking nonsense.
  你有什么毛病啊？不要一直讲一堆没用的。

- Please don't hesitate to contact us if you have any further **problem**.
  如果你有任何其他的问题，请不要犹豫，马上与我们联络。

**美国人常用短语**

- **bring about** 引起
- **to one's annoyance** 令人生气的是
- **come across** 偶然发现
- **make a fuss** 小题大做
- **traffic jam** 堵车
- **a tight corner / spot** 困境
- **in a pickle** 陷入困境

# 英语的逻辑——30天学会美国人的英语逻辑

## 相关词汇群组记忆

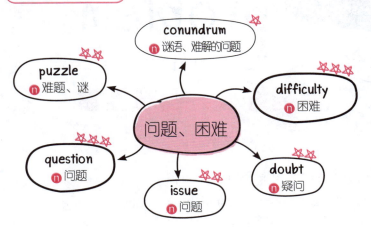

- **conundrum**
  [kə'nʌndrəm]
  n 谜语、难解的问题

  This is the most complicated conundrum I've ever come across.
  这是我遇见过的最复杂的谜语。

- **difficulty**
  ['dɪfɪkəlti]
  n 困难

  I believe I have the courage to break through difficulties in life.
  我相信我有勇气克服生命中的困境。
  → break through 表示"克服、突破障碍"

- **doubt**
  [daʊt]
  n 疑问

  Don't you have any doubts about his decision?
  你对他的决定没有任何疑虑吗?

- **issue**
  ['ɪʃu]
  n 问题

  Viola and I like to talk about political issues over coffee.
  薇欧拉和我喜欢边喝咖啡边聊政治问题。

- **question**
  ['kwestʃən]
  n 问题

  Many students rarely ask questions in class.
  许多学生很少在课堂上提问。

- **puzzle**
  ['pʌzl]
  n 难题、谜

  I like to play crossword puzzles very much.
  我很喜欢玩填字游戏。

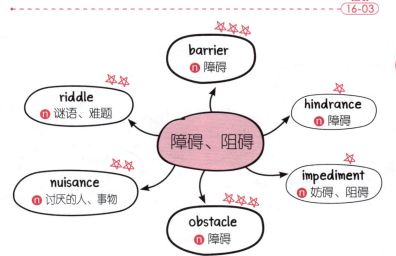

- **barrier**
  ['bæriər]
  n 障碍

  His lack of confidence became a barrier to having a successful interpersonal relationship.
  他缺乏自信心，这成为拥有成功的人际关系的障碍。

- **hindrance**
  ['hɪndrəns]
  n 障碍

  My washing machine was mended and it can run without hindrance.
  我的洗衣机修理好了，可以顺利运转。

- **impediment**
  [ɪm'pedɪmənt]
  n 妨碍、阻碍

  Over-parenting could be an impediment to child development.
  过度管教可能会阻碍孩子的发展。

- **obstacle**
  ['ɑːbstəkl]
  n 障碍

  I will break through all the obstacles to become successful.
  我会突破所有阻挠我成功的障碍。

- **nuisance**
  ['nuːsns]
  n 讨厌的人、事物

  My neighbor's dog is a total nuisance.
  我邻居的狗真令人讨厌。

- **riddle**
  ['rɪdl]
  n 谜语、难题

  Solving lantern riddles is a traditional custom of the Lantern Festival.
  猜灯谜是元宵节的一项传统习俗。

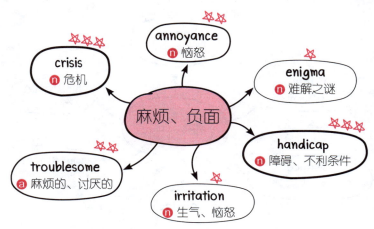

- **annoyance**
  [əˈnɔɪəns]
  n 恼怒

  To my annoyance, my husband was driving the wrong way.
  令我生气的是，我丈夫开错路了。

- **enigma**
  [ɪˈnɪɡmə]
  n 难解之谜

  To some people, Lucy's whereabouts is still an enigma.
  对某些人来说，露西的下落仍然是个谜团。
  → whereabouts 表示"下落、行踪"

- **handicap**
  [ˈhændɪkæp]
  n 障碍、不利条件

  I had quite a few handicaps to overcome when I first learned to surf.
  我一开始学冲浪的时候，必须克服一些障碍。

- **irritation**
  [ˌɪrɪˈteɪʃn]
  n 生气、恼怒

  My irritation with my roommate is growing stronger.
  我对我的室友越来越恼怒。

- **troublesome**
  [ˈtrʌblsəm]
  a 麻烦的、讨厌的

  The traffic jam is really troublesome.
  交通堵塞真是令人讨厌。 → traffic jam 表示"交通堵塞"

- **crisis**
  [ˈkraɪsɪs]
  n 危机

  Food crisis is a major concern for many countries.
  粮食危机是很多国家主要关切的事项。

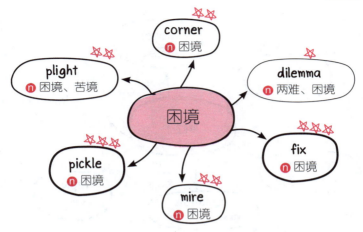

- **corner**
  ['kɔrnər]
  n 困境

  Don't lose hope when you are in a tight corner.
  当你处在困境时，别放弃希望。→ a tight corner / spot 表示"困境"

- **dilemma**
  [dɪ'lemə]
  n 两难、困境

  Should I eat braised pork rice or beef noodle for lunch? It's such a dilemma.
  午餐要吃卤肉饭还是牛肉面？真是两难。

- **fix**
  [fɪks]
  n 困境

  Will was broke. He was in a fix.
  威尔破产了，他陷入了困境。

- **mire**
  ['maɪər]
  n 困境

  The factory closed and the workers were in the mire.
  工厂倒闭，工人处于困境中。

- **pickle**
  ['pɪkl]
  n 困境

  I was in a pickle when I was fired from my job.
  我失业时陷入了困境。→ in a pickle 表示"陷入困境"

- **plight**
  [plaɪt]
  n 困境、苦境

  The plight of famine in Somalia has been severe in recent years.
  索马里的饥荒困境在近几年一直非常严重。
  → famine 表示"饥荒"；severe 表示"严重的"

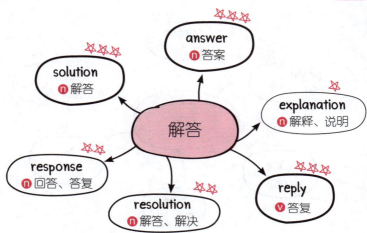

- **answer**
  [ˈænsər]
  n 答案

  No one has answers to everything.
  没有人能回答所有问题。

- **explanation**
  [ˌɛksplə'neɪʃn]
  n 解释、说明

  Dr. Liu is giving a clear explanation of why dinosaurs became extinct.
  刘博士对于恐龙灭绝的原因，正给予一个清楚的解释。
  → extinct 表示"灭绝的、绝种的"

- **reply**
  [rɪ'plaɪ]
  v 答复

  Please reply to me as soon as possible.
  请尽快给我答复。

- **resolution**
  [ˌrɛzə'luʃn]
  n 解答、解决

  We held a meeting to find out the resolution to the problem.
  我们召开会议以便找出问题的解决方案。

- **response**
  [rɪ'spɑns]
  n 回答、答复

  He frowned in response to my question.
  他把皱眉当作对我的问题的回应。 → frown 表示"皱眉头"

- **solution**
  [sə'luʃn]
  n 解答

  Can you figure out the best solution to this problem?
  你能想出这个问题的最佳解决方案吗？

# Lesson 17

# serious

['sɪriəs]

## 了解事情的严重性

💬 **serious** 形容词表示"严重的、危险的、严肃的、重要的、认真的、感兴趣的"。

- I'm not kidding. This is a very serious matter.
  我不是开玩笑,这件事情非常严重。

- My boss always looks collected and serious.
  我的老板总是看起来很冷静且严肃。

- I'm serious about being a war photographer.
  我对于当一名战地摄影师是很认真的。

- Don't look so serious; he is just kidding.
  别这么严肃,他只是在开玩笑。

- I'm serious about this, and I need your support.
  我对这件事情是非常认真的,而且我需要你的支持。

**美国人常用短语**

- **think over** 仔细思考
- **not in the least** 一点也不
- **turn off** 关掉
- **get along with** 与……和睦相处
- **focus on** 集中于

## 相关词汇群组记忆

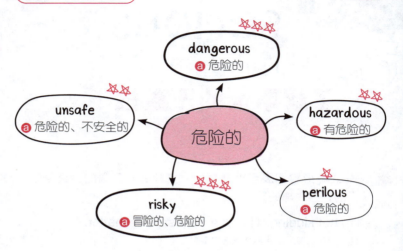

- **dangerous**
  ['deɪndʒərəs]
  ⓐ 危险的

  Drunk driving is very dangerous.
  酒后驾车是非常危险的。

- **hazardous**
  ['hæzərdəs]
  ⓐ 有危险的

  Trans fat is hazardous to our health.
  反式脂肪有害健康。　→ trans fat 表示"反式脂肪"

- **perilous**
  ['perələs]
  ⓐ 危险的

  The ship navigated a perilous sea filled with icebergs.
  那艘船航行于充满冰山的危险海域。　→ navigate 表示"航行"

- **risky**
  ['rɪski]
  ⓐ 冒险的、危险的

  It's risky to ride a motorcycle without a helmet.
  骑摩托车不戴安全帽很危险。

- **unsafe**
  [ʌn'seɪf]
  ⓐ 危险的、不安全的

  It's unsafe to go climbing alone.
  独自登山不安全。

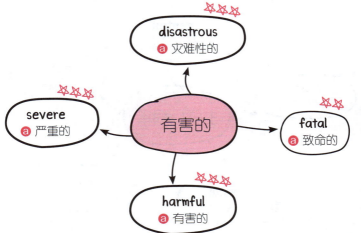

- ▶ **disastrous**
  [dɪ'zæstrəs]
  ⓐ 灾难性的

  Yesterday, a disastrous avalanche occurred that killed ten people.
  昨天发生了一场灾难性的雪崩导致了十个人死亡。
  → avalanche 表示"雪崩"

- ▶ **fatal**
  ['feɪtl]
  ⓐ 致命的

  Acquired Immune Deficiency Syndrome (AIDS) is a fatal disease.
  获得性免疫缺陷综合征（艾滋病）是一种致命的疾病。
  → acquired 表示"获得的"；immune 表示"免疫的"；deficiency 表示"缺陷"；syndrome 表示"综合征"

- ▶ **harmful**
  ['hɑːrmfl]
  ⓐ 有害的

  Losing weight too fast could be harmful to your health.
  减重太快可能有害健康。

- ▶ **severe**
  [sɪ'vɪr]
  ⓐ 严重的

  Peter had severe knee pain after running.
  彼得跑步之后膝盖剧烈疼痛。

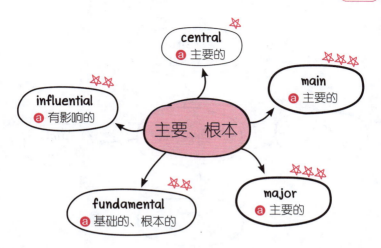

- **central**
  [ˈsentrəl]
  ⓐ 主要的

  The two central concepts of this book are natural selection and survival of the fittest.
  这本书的两个主要概念是自然淘汰与适者生存。
  → survival 表示"生存"；fittest 表示"最适合的"

- **main**
  [meɪn]
  ⓐ 主要的

  One of the main ingredients of this dish is saffron.
  这道菜的主要原料之一是藏红花。
  → ingredient 表示"原料、组成部分"；saffron 表示"藏红花"

- **major**
  [ˈmeɪdʒər]
  ⓐ 主要的

  Can you tell the major difference between American and British English?
  你能分辨美式英语与英式英语的主要差别吗？

- **fundamental**
  [ˌfʌndəˈmentl]
  ⓐ 基础的、根本的

  The fundamental problem of this project is money.
  这项计划的根本问题是钱。

- **influential**
  [ˌɪnfluˈenʃl]
  ⓐ 有影响的

  Can you name some influential historical figures of China?
  你能列举一些中国有影响力的历史人物吗？

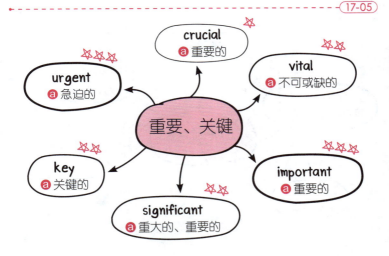

► **crucial**
['kruʃl]
ⓐ 重要的

A healthy diet is crucial to everyone.
健康饮食对每个人都很重要。

► **vital**
['vaɪtl]
ⓐ 不可或缺的

Composition and light are vital elements for a good photograph.
构图与光线是一张好的照片不可或缺的要素。
→ composition 表示"构图、结构"

► **important**
[ɪm'pɔrtnt]
ⓐ 重要的

It's important that we should respect cultural differences.
重要的是我们应该尊重文化差异。

► **significant**
[sɪg'nɪfɪkənt]
ⓐ 重大的、重要的

This new drug has a significant impact to health.
这个新药品对健康有重大影响。

► **key**
[kiː]
ⓐ 关键的

The key point of this story is about the loss of innocence.
本故事的重点是关于纯真的丧失。

► **urgent**
['ɜrdʒnt]
ⓐ 急迫的

This temple is in urgent need of renovation.
这座庙急需修缮。 → renovation 表示"整修、翻新"

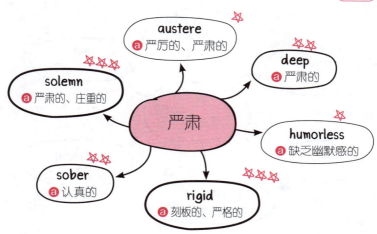

- **austere**
  [ɔ'stɪr]
  ⓐ 严厉的、严肃的

  My piano teacher is very strict and austere.
  我的钢琴老师非常严格且严厉。

- **deep**
  [dip]
  ⓐ 严肃的

  This is a deep problem. I have to think it over.
  这是个严肃的问题。我必须仔细想一想。

- **humorless**
  ['hjumərlɪs]
  ⓐ 缺乏幽默感的

  How come a young man like you is old-fashioned and humorless?
  像你这样的年轻人怎么会古板又没幽默感呢？

- **rigid**
  ['rɪdʒɪd]
  ⓐ 刻板的、严格的

  Although Professor Gordon is highly-esteemed in academic circles, he is very rigid in his point of view.
  虽然高登教授在学术界备受推崇，他却僵化于自己的观点。

- **sober**
  ['soubər]
  ⓐ 认真的

  He is very sober and self-disciplined. He sleeps only for four hours a day.
  他非常认真且自律，每天只睡四个小时。

- **solemn**
  ['sɑləm]
  ⓐ 严肃的、庄重的

  Everyone attending the funeral looked so grave and solemn.
  参加葬礼的每个人看起来都很严肃且庄重。

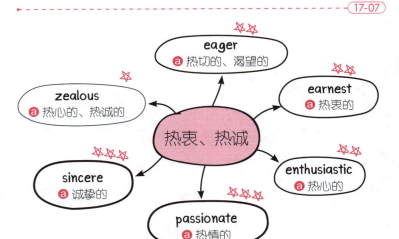

- ▶ **eager**
  ['igər]
  ⓐ 热切的、渴望的

  He is eager to be a billionaire.
  他渴望成为亿万富翁。

- ▶ **earnest**
  ['ɜrnɪst]
  ⓐ 热衷的

  He is earnest about making money.
  他热衷于赚钱。

- ▶ **enthusiastic**
  [ɪnˌθuzɪ'æstɪk]
  ⓐ 热心的

  Joy is enthusiastic about doing volunteer work.
  乔伊热心于做志愿者工作。

- ▶ **passionate**
  ['pæʃənət]
  ⓐ 热情的

  Dwight is very passionate about playing basketball.
  德怀特对于打篮球很有热情。

- ▶ **sincere**
  [sɪn'sɪr]
  ⓐ 诚挚的

  She is not in the least sincere.
  她一点儿也不诚挚。 → not in the least 表示"一点儿也不"

- ▶ **zealous**
  ['zeləs]
  ⓐ 热心的、热诚的

  My mother is a zealous Buddhist. She reads the Buddhist scripture every morning.
  我的妈妈是一位热诚的佛教徒。她每天早上都念佛经。

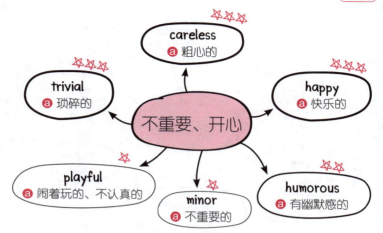

▶ **careless**
['kerləs]
ⓐ 粗心的

I forgot to turn off the lights before leaving. I was so careless.
我离开前忘了关灯。我真粗心。　→ turn off 表示"关掉"

▶ **happy**
['hæpi]
ⓐ 快乐的

Why do all the fairy tales have happy endings?
为什么所有童话故事都有快乐的结局？

▶ **humorous**
['hjumərəs]
ⓐ 有幽默感的

She is so humorous. She can get along with everybody.
她很有幽默感。她可以跟每个人相处得融洽。

▶ **minor**
['maɪnər]
ⓐ 不重要的

This is just a minor problem. We don't need to worry about it.
这是个不重要的问题，我们无须担心。

▶ **playful**
['pleɪfl]
ⓐ 闹着玩的、不认真的

Evelyn gave me a playful wink.
伊芙琳俏皮地向我眨眨眼。
→ wink 表示"眨眼"

▶ **trivial**
['trɪviəl]
ⓐ 琐碎的

We should focus on the big picture, not trivial things.
我们应该着眼于大局，而非琐事。

# Lesson 18

# use

v [juz]  n [juz]

## 了解用途，善加利用

🔴 **use** 动词表示"使用、利用、运用"；
名词表示"使用、用途"。

- My ninety-year-old grandfather knows how to **use** a smartphone.
  我九十岁的祖父知道怎么用智能手机。

- Sometimes words can be **used** as weapons to protect or to harm people.
  有时候文字被用作武器来保护或者伤害人们。

- You have to make good **use** of this opportunity to apply your talent.
  你必须充分利用这次机会发挥所长。 → make use of 表示"利用"

- Can you show me how to **use** this tool?
  你可以教我怎么使用这个工具吗？

- I can't believe you let her **use** your toothbrush; it's disgusting.
  我不能相信你让她用你的牙刷，真恶心。

- **make use of** 利用
- **help out** 帮助解决问题

## 相关词汇群组记忆

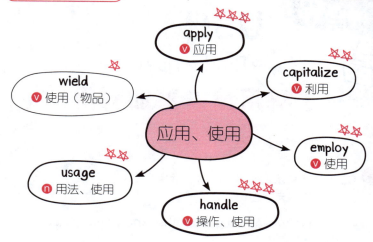

- **apply**
  [ə'plaɪ]
  v 应用

  It's not easy to apply educational theories to the classroom.
  要将教育理论应用到课堂中是很不容易的。

- **capitalize**
  ['kæpɪtəlaɪz]
  v 利用

  We should capitalize on this great opportunity to make a fortune.
  我们应该利用这大好机会赚大钱。

- **employ**
  [ɪm'plɔɪ]
  v 使用

  The teacher employed Audio-lingual Method in teaching English.
  老师使用"听说教学法"来教英语。 → audio 表示"听觉的"

- **handle**
  ['hændl]
  v 操作、使用

  He learned how to handle an excavator today.
  他今天学习如何操作挖土机。 → excavator 表示"挖土机"

- **usage**
  ['jusɪdʒ]
  n 用法、使用

  I'm reading the usage instructions of the product.
  我正在读产品的使用说明书。

- **wield**
  [wild]
  v 使用（物品）

  A man wielding a knife was approaching a woman standing on the platform.
  一个持刀的男子逐渐靠近一个站在月台上的女子。

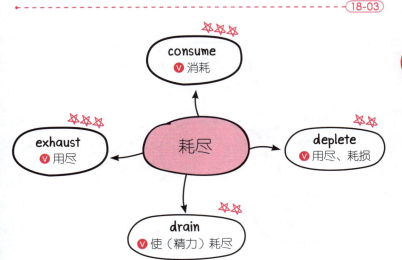

- ▶ **consume**
  [kən'sum]
  Ⓥ 消耗

  Many people consume most of their time in using social media.
  许多人耗费大部分时间使用社交媒体。

- ▶ **deplete**
  [dɪ'plit]
  Ⓥ 用尽、耗损

  Most natural forests in this region have been depleted.
  这个地区大部分的天然森林已被耗尽。

- ▶ **drain**
  [dreɪn]
  Ⓥ 使（精力）耗尽

  I was drained and fell asleep.
  我感到精疲力竭，就睡着了。

- ▶ **exhaust**
  [ɪg'zɔst]
  Ⓥ 用尽

  I was so exhausted after working out for two hours.
  健身两小时后，我觉得精疲力竭。
  → work out 表示"健身"

- **abuse**
  [ə'bjus]
  n 滥用

  Drug abuse causes serious social problems.
  药物滥用会导致严重的社会问题。

- **exploit**
  [ɪk'splɔɪt]
  v 剥削

  This policy is aimed to prevent laborers from being exploited.
  这项政策的目的在于避免劳工被剥削。

- **misuse**
  [ˌmɪs'jus]
  v 滥用、误用

  Antibiotics are often misused in treating illnesses.
  在治疗疾病中抗生素经常被滥用。
  → antibiotics 表示"抗生素"

- **waste**
  [weɪst]
  v 浪费

  I never waste time on something meaningless.
  我从不浪费时间在无意义的事情上。

- **squander**
  ['skwandər]
  v 浪费

  Don't squander time because life is short.
  别浪费光阴,因为生命很短暂。

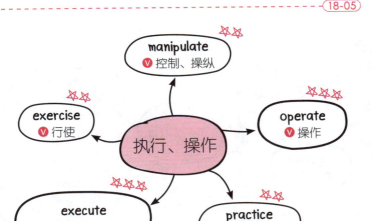

- **manipulate**
  [məˈnɪpjuleɪt]
  Ⓥ 控制、操纵

  She is pretty good at manipulating people to get what she wants.
  她非常擅长操控别人以达到她的目的。
  → good at 表示"擅长"

- **operate**
  [ˈɑpəreɪt]
  Ⓥ 操作

  If you operate the machine improperly, an accident might occur.
  如果你操作机器不当，可能就会发生意外。

- **practice**
  [ˈpræktɪs]
  Ⓥ 实践、实行

  Most families make ends meet by practicing how to save and keep a budget.
  大部分的家庭实行省钱与预算安排以达到收支平衡。
  → make ends meet 表示"收支平衡"

- **execute**
  [ˈeksɪkjut]
  Ⓥ 实施、履行、执行

  The new promotion strategies will be executed next month.
  新的宣传策略将于下个月实施。

- **exercise**
  [ˈeksərsaɪz]
  Ⓥ 行使

  We should exercise our rights properly.
  我们应适当地行使我们的权利。

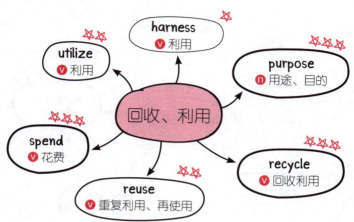

▶ **harness**
['hɑːrnɪs]
v 利用

Today we're going to learn how solar energy is **harnessed** to generate electricity.
今天我们要学习太阳能是如何被用来发电的。

▶ **purpose**
['pɜːrpəs]
n 用途、目的

The **purpose** of technology is to create a better life.
科技的目的是创造更好的生活。

▶ **recycle**
[ˌriˈsaɪkl]
v 回收利用

These used clothes can be **recycled** or sent to the charity.
这些旧衣服可被回收或是寄到慈善机构。

▶ **reuse**
[ˌriˈjuːs]
v 重复利用、再使用

**Reusing** needles can lead to high risk of infection.
重复使用针头会有高度感染风险。 → infection 表示"感染"

▶ **spend**
[spend]
v 花费

I **spend** half an hour doing the dishes every day.
我每天花半小时洗碗。

▶ **utilize**
['jutəlaɪz]
v 利用

You must **utilize** your talent properly in your career.
你必须在事业上适当发挥你的才能。

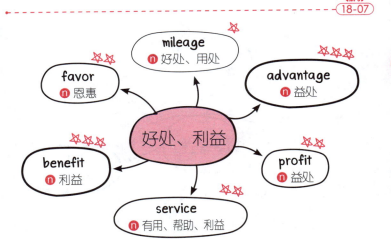

- **mileage**
  ['maɪlɪdʒ]
  n 好处、用处

  I've already gotten a lot of mileage out of my cellphone; it's so reliable!
  我已经得到了手机带来的许多好处。

- **advantage**
  [əd'væntɪdʒ]
  n 益处

  There are many advantages in learning martial arts.
  学习武术有许多好处。 → martial art 表示"武术"

- **profit**
  ['prɑfɪt]
  n 益处

  What profit can I get from eating dark chocolate?
  吃黑巧克力对我有什么益处？

- **service**
  ['sɜrvɪs]
  n 有用、帮助、利益

  Thank you for fixing my laptop. You did me a great service.
  谢谢你帮我修理我的笔记本电脑。你帮了我一个大忙。

- **benefit**
  ['bɛnɪfɪt]
  n 利益

  This invention is expected to bring benefit to all of mankind.
  这项发明预计将为全人类带来利益。

- **favor**
  ['feɪvər]
  n 恩惠

  Could you do me a favor? I need someone to give me a ride home.
  你能帮我一个忙吗？我需要有人载我回家。

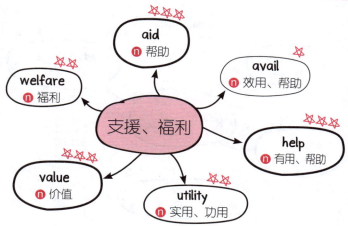

- **aid**
  [eɪd]
  n 帮助

  The victims in this earthquake needed financial aid.
  这次地震的灾民需要财政援助。

- **avail**
  [əˈveɪl]
  n 效用、帮助

  The suspect tried to escape from the handcuffs but to no avail.
  嫌犯试图挣脱手铐，但是没有奏效。
  → handcuff 表示"手铐"；to no avail 表示"毫无效果"

- **help**
  [help]
  n 有用、帮助

  Thank you for helping me out. You've been a lot of help.
  谢谢你帮我解决问题，真是帮了我大忙。
  → help out 表示"帮助解决问题"

- **utility**
  [juˈtɪləti]
  n 实用、功用

  The utility of nutritional supplements remain controversy.
  保健食品的功效仍受到争议。 → nutritional 表示"营养的"

- **value**
  [ˈvælju]
  n 价值

  The value of friendship is hard to measure.
  友情的价值难以衡量。

- **welfare**
  [ˈwelfer]
  n 福利

  The fundraising was held for the welfare of stray dogs.
  这次募款活动是为了流浪狗的福利而举办的。

# 美国人聊天都说这些话

## Part 3

## Lesson 19  You're Getting on My Nerves

## 你惹毛我了

如果有人令你感到"很生气",那么如何用英语表达呢?

就是"You're getting on my nerves"。nerve是"神经"的意思。这句字面上的解释是"你触碰到我的神经了",引申为"你让我不高兴""你让我生气了""你让我很心烦"或者"你把我惹毛了"。因此,当某人或某事令你感到不快或者厌烦时,即可使用"get on my nerves"这个短语。

- You're really getting on my nerves. You'd better stop.
  你实在令我很生气,你最好停止。

- That construction noise really gets on my nerves.
  施工噪声真令我受不了。

- Quit shaking your legs. You're getting on my nerves.
  不要再抖腿了,真的令我很烦。

- Stop singing. You're getting on my nerves.
  别再唱了,我好心烦。

- Her rudeness gets on my nerves.
  她的粗鲁令我生气。

- It gets on my nerves that she's been bad-mouthing me.
  令我生气的是,她一直在说我坏话。
  ↳ bad-mouth 表示"说别人坏话"

(相关会话群组记忆) 表达"生气、不高兴、愤怒、厌烦"

19-02

★ I'm not happy. ……………………………………… 我不高兴。
★ I'm angry. / I feel angry.
  ……………………………… 我很生气。/ 我觉得很生气。
★ I'm upset. ………………………………………… 我很心烦。
★ I'm mad.  → mad 的生气程度大于 angry ………… 我很愤怒。
★ I'm annoyed. …………………………………… 我很气恼。
★ I'm furious. ……………………………………… 我感到愤怒。
  → furious 表示"极度愤怒"
★ I'm irritated. …………………………………… 我很恼火。
★ I'm peeved. ……………………………………… 我感到恼怒。
  → peeve 表示"使恼怒";peeved 表示"恼怒的"
★ I'm fuming. ……………………………………… 我发怒了。
★ I'm outraged. ………………………………… 我觉得很愤慨。
  → outrage 表示"使震怒";outraged 表示"强烈感到震惊与愤怒"
★ I was livid. ……………………………………… 我非常愤怒。

19-03

★ I'm not happy about it. / I'm unhappy about it.
  ………………………………………………… 我对此感到不高兴。
★ I'm angry at / with you. ………………… 你令我很生气。
★ I'm angry about it. ……………………… 我对此很生气。
★ I'm mad at you. …………………………… 你令我感到愤怒。
★ I'm mad about it. ………………………… 我对这件事很愤怒。
★ I'm irritated by his manner. ………… 他的态度令我感到恼怒。
★ I'm irritated at it. ………………………… 我对此感到恼怒。
★ He is furious at it. ……………………… 他对此感到愤怒。

★ He is furious with me. ……他对我感到愤怒。
★ I'm in a temper. ……我正在气头上。
   ↳ temper 表示"脾气"；in a temper 表示"发脾气"
★ I lost my temper. ……我生气了。
★ I'm in a bad / foul temper. ……我发脾气了。
   ↳ foul 表示"很糟的、不愉快的"
★ He has a hot / short / quick temper. ……他脾气暴躁。
★ He is bad / hot / ill / short / quick-tempered.
   ……他脾气暴躁。
★ She is in a foul mood. ……她心情不好。
★ I was livid about it. ……我对此感到暴怒。
★ She was cross with me. ……她生我的气。
   ↳ cross 表示"生气的"

19-04

★ I'm sick of it. ……我受够了。
★ I'm sick and tired of it. ……我受够了也厌烦透了。
★ I'm fed up with it. ……我受够了。
   ↳ fed up with... 表示"受够……了"
★ That's enough! ……够了！
★ Mind your own business! ……别多管闲事！
★ I can't stand it anymore! ……我再也受不了了！
★ You're bothering me. ……你让我很烦。
★ It gets to me. ……这让我很生气。
   ↳ get to sb. 表示"令……生气"
★ It winds me up. ……这让我很生气。
★ I'm getting worked up. ……我生气了。
★ I'm pissed off. ……我很生气。
   ↳ piss off 表示"使生气"
★ That's too much. ……那太过分了。
★ You're going too far. / That's going too far.
   ……你太过分了。/ 那太过分了。

### 听美国人聊天

**A** You look so angry. What's going on?
你看起来很生气,怎么了?

**B** I had a fight with my boyfriend last night.
我昨天晚上跟男朋友吵架了。

---

**A** I failed the driving test three times. 我驾照考了三次都没过。

**B** Don't be upset. 别懊恼了。

---

**A** I'm getting worked up. 我生气了。

**B** Just calm down. 冷静下来。

---

**A** Today's game was rained out. 今天的比赛因雨延期。

**B** I'm unhappy about it. 真令人不开心。

---

**A** You shouldn't have said that. That's going too far.
你不该那么说,那太过分了。

**B** I'm sorry. I didn't mean it. 对不起,我不是有意的。

---

**A** I got a ticket. 我被开罚单了。

**B** What a nuisance! 真是讨厌!

---

**A** Susan really made me so mad. 苏珊真的令我很生气。

**B** Take it easy. What happened? 别生气了。怎么了?

**A** I can't believe she took it out on me for no reason.
我不敢相信她毫无理由地拿我出气。

**B** That's just too much! 那真是太过分了!

---

**A** How was your weekend? 周末过得如何?

**B** I was annoyed because the air conditioner didn't work.
很烦,因为空调坏了。

(相关会话群组记忆) 表达"高兴、快乐、愉快、心情好"

19-05

★ **Good / Great.** ……………………………… 太好了。
★ **Nice.** ……………………………… 真好。
★ **That's terrific / incredible / fantastic / wonderful / marvelous!** ……………………………… 太棒了!

19-06

★ I'm so happy. ……………………………… 我很快乐。
★ I feel good / great. ……………………………… 我感觉很好。
★ I'm in a good mood. ……………………………… 我心情很好。
★ I feel blessed. ……………………………… 我觉得很快乐。
★ He is such a jolly guy. ……………………………… 他是这么一个快乐的人。
★ What a pleasant day. ……………………………… 真是愉快的一天。
★ I'm content with my life. ……………………………… 我对我的生活很满意。
　　content 表示"满意的"
★ I couldn't be happier. ……………………………… 我十分高兴。
★ It's too good to be true. ……………………………… 这简直太好了。
★ You look cheerful. ……………………………… 你看起来很高兴。
★ I feel so lighthearted. ……………………………… 我感到心情愉快。

19-07

★ I'm over the moon about it. ……………………………… 我为此欣喜若狂。
★ I'm thrilled to bits. ……………………………… 我高兴极了。
　　thrilled to bits 表示"高兴极了"
★ I'm in seventh heaven. ……………………………… 我高兴极了。
★ I'm on cloud nine. 较口语 ……………………………… 我乐不可支。
★ I'm so stoked. ……………………………… 我很振奋。
★ I'm happy as a clam. ……………………………… 我相当幸福。

## 听美国人聊天

**A** I'm getting married. 我要结婚了。
**B** Congratulations! I'm happy for you. 恭喜！我替你感到开心。

---

**A** I have found an ideal job. 我找到理想的工作了。
**B** That's fantastic! 太棒了！

---

**A** How are you doing? 你过得如何？
**B** I feel great. 我觉得很好。

---

**A** I've been having a hard time recently. 我最近日子不好过。
**B** Cheer up! Everything will be fine. 振作起来！一切都会好的。

---

**A** I just got a promotion and a raise. 我刚升迁而且又加薪。
**B** No wonder you're over the moon. 怪不得你那么高兴。

---

**A** Linda's fiance is handsome, young and rich.
琳达的未婚夫又帅、又年轻、又有钱。
**B** It's too good to be true. 简直好得难以置信。

---

**A** How's your new car? 你的新车怎么样？
**B** Great. I'm pleased with it. 很棒，我很满意。

---

**A** You look good in that dress. 你穿那件连衣裙很好看。
**B** Thank you. You just made my day. 谢谢，你这么说我很高兴。

---

**A** How's your retired life going? 你退休生活过得如何？
**B** I'm happy as a clam. 我过得很快活。

---

**A** Do you like working out? 你喜欢健身吗？
**B** Yes. I get a kick out of it. 喜欢，从中我获得许多乐趣。

Part 3 美国人聊天都说这些话

**美国人还会这样说** 其他与表达"生气"相关的惯用语

## 1. hit the ceiling 勃然大怒

hit 是"撞击",ceiling 是"天花板",hit the ceiling 字面上的意思是"撞到天花板",但实际意思跟天花板并没有关系,而是"勃然大怒"的意思。

- She hit the ceiling when she found her son stole money from her.
  当她发现她儿子偷她的钱时,她勃然大怒。

## 2. go through the roof 大发雷霆

roof 是"屋顶",go through the roof 字面上的意思是"穿过屋顶",引申为"暴跳如雷""大发雷霆"的意思。

- I will go through the roof if you do that again.
  如果你再那么做,我就会大发雷霆。

## 3. hot under the collar 非常愤怒

hot 是"很热",collar"衣领"。under the collar 意思是"衣领下方",也就是脖子的部位。hot under the collar 字面上的意思是"衣领下方很热",也就是脖子部位很热。表示一个人生气到脖子发烫,可引申为"非常愤怒""怒火中烧"的意思。

- I was hot under the collar when I knew my mother read my diary.
  当我知道我母亲看我的日记时,我非常愤怒。

# Lesson 20 There Is No Accounting for Tastes

## 人各有喜好

Part 3 美国人聊天都说这些话

> 中文"人各有喜好",英语要如何表达呢?

就是"There is no accounting for tastes"。account for 是动词短语,是"解释、说明"的意思。taste 是"爱好、喜欢"的意思。这句字面上解释是"无法解释爱好""爱好是无法解释的",也就是"人各有喜好/所好"的意思。因此,当你要表达每个人有不同的兴趣、不同的品位时,可使用"There is no accounting for tastes"。

- **There is no accounting for tastes.** Cooking is not my cup of tea.

  人各有喜好,烹饪并非我所爱。
  ↪ sb.'s cup of tea 表示"某人喜爱的事物"

- "Why did he marry her?" **"There is no accounting for tastes."**

  "他为什么娶她?""人各有喜好。"

- **There is no accounting for tastes.** Although carrots are rich in beta-carotene, I never eat carrots.

  人各有喜好。虽然胡萝卜富含 β 胡萝卜素,我却从不吃胡萝卜。

- **There is no accounting for tastes.** I like you the best.

  人各有喜好,我最喜欢你。

（相关会话群组记忆） 表达"喜欢、想要、希望"

20-02

★ **I like it.** 任何情况皆适用 ………………… 我喜欢。
★ **I like spaghetti.** ………………… 我喜欢意大利面。
★ **I like high heels.** ………………… 我喜欢高跟鞋。
★ **I like jogging.** ………………… 我喜欢慢跑。
★ **I like to play the piano.** ………………… 我喜欢弹钢琴。
★ **I love coffee.** ………………… 我热爱咖啡。
★ **I love painting.** ………………… 我爱画画。
★ **Do you fancy some tea?** ………………… 你想要喝些茶吗？
★ **I fancy dancing.** ………………… 我喜欢跳舞。
　　fancy 表示"想要、喜欢"
★ **I enjoyed this concert.** ………………… 我很喜欢这场演唱会。
★ **I enjoy listening to music.** ………………… 我喜爱听音乐。
★ **I want to be a millionaire.** ………………… 我想成为百万富翁。
★ **I wish to travel the world.** ………………… 我想要环游世界。

20-03

★ I'm crazy about you. ………………… 我为你着迷。
★ Mike is crazy about extreme sports.
　………………… 迈克很热衷于极限运动。
★ My boyfriend is mad about online games.
　………………… 我男朋友着迷于线上游戏。
★ I'm fond of you. ………………… 我喜欢你。
★ I'm fond of reading. ………………… 我喜欢阅读。
　　be fond of 表示"喜欢"
★ He's my kind of guy. ………………… 他是我喜欢的类型。
★ I'm interested. ………………… 我很有兴趣。

★ I am pleased. ……………………………………… 我很满意。
★ It was fun. ………………………………………… 这真有趣。
★ I like boxing best. ……………………………… 我最喜欢拳击。
★ I fell for him at first sight. …………………… 我对他一见钟情。
  ↳ fall for 表示"迷恋"
★ Do you like opera? ……………………………… 你喜欢歌剧吗？
★ He goes for women with long hair. ……… 他喜欢长发女子。
  ↳ go for 表示"喜欢"
★ I'm happy with my new job. …………… 我对我的新工作感到开心。
★ I'm satisfied with it. …………………………… 我对此很满意。
★ This is so exciting. …………………………… 这真令人兴奋。
★ I'm keen on fishing. ………………………… 我热爱钓鱼。
★ I'm partial to jazz. …………………………… 我偏爱爵士乐。
  ↳ partial to 表示"偏爱"
★ She chose biology as her major. …… 她选择生物学作为专业。
★ She yearns to be a chef. ……………… 她渴望成为一名大厨。
★ Prisoners pine for freedom. ………………… 囚犯渴望自由。
  ↳ pine for 表示"渴望得到"
★ He longs for a successful career. 他渴望拥有成功的事业。
★ I am eager for happiness. …………………… 我渴望快乐。
★ I hunger for adventures. …………………… 我渴望冒险。
★ I'm so into archeology. ……………… 我对考古学很感兴趣。
  ↳ into sth. 表示"对……很感兴趣"
★ I thirst for knowledge. ……………………… 我渴求知识。
★ I aspire to be a movie star. …………… 我向往成为电影明星。
★ People aspire for peace. …………………… 人们向往和平。
★ He started to take to this song. ……… 他开始喜欢上这首歌。
  ↳ take to 表示"喜欢上"
★ The thing I prize most is honesty. … 我最重视的事是诚实。
  ↳ prize 表示"珍惜、重视"

Part 3 美国人聊天都说这些话

★ I cherish our friendship. ……………… 我珍惜我们的友谊。
★ I treasure the moment we spent together.
　…………………………………………… 我珍惜我们相处的时光。
★ I truly appreciate your wisdom. ……… 我真的欣赏你的智慧。
★ I esteem you greatly. ………………………… 我非常尊敬你。

------------------------------------------------ 20-04

★ I prefer winter to summer. ………………… 我喜欢冬天胜过夏天。
★ I revel in classical music. ………………………… 我着迷于古典乐。
　↳ revel in 表示"着迷于"
★ I prefer not to tell him the truth. ………… 我选择不告诉他真相。
★ I have a preference for horror movies. ……… 我偏好恐怖电影。
★ She delights in playing pranks on friends. …… 她以开朋友玩笑为乐。
　↳ prank 表示"玩笑、恶作剧"；delight in 表示"以……为乐"。
★ I have a weakness for cakes. ………………… 我对蛋糕有所偏好。
　↳ weakness 除了"弱点"之外，在这里指的是"偏爱"。
★ I prefer drinking water to drinking tea. ………… 我喜欢喝水胜过喝茶。
★ I prefer to walk (rather) than to drive. ………… 我喜欢走路胜过开车。
★ Camille Claudel is my favorite sculptress.
　………………………………… 卡米耶·克洛岱尔是我最喜欢的女雕刻家。
★ I relish riding my bike. ……………………… 我喜欢骑我的自行车。
　↳ relish 表示"喜欢、爱好"
★ I relish competition. ………………………………… 我享受竞争。
★ Ang Lee is the film director I admire most.
　…………………………………………… 李安是我最钦佩的电影导演。
★ I adore him for his integrity. ……………… 我因为他的正直而敬重他。
★ I became addicted to photography. ……………… 我迷上摄影了。
★ I prefer short hair. …………………………………… 我偏好短发。
★ I usually crave for dessert after a meal. …… 通常饭后我都想吃甜点。
　↳ crave 表示"渴望"
★ I have a soft spot for my niece. ……………… 我特别喜欢我侄女。
　↳ have a soft spot for 表示"偏爱、对……有好感"

**听美国人聊天**

- **A** Who's your favorite actor? 你最喜欢的演员是谁？
- **B** Robert De Niro is my favorite actor.
  我最喜欢的演员是罗伯特·德尼罗。

---

- **A** Do you want me to drive you home? 要不要我载你回家？
- **B** No, thanks. I prefer walking home.
  不了，谢谢。我比较想走路回家。

---

- **A** I have a sweet tooth. I love to have dessert after a meal.
  我爱吃甜食。我喜欢在饭后吃甜点。 → have a sweet tooth 表示"爱吃甜食"
- **B** Me too. I especially love chocolate cakes.
  我也是，我特别喜爱巧克力蛋糕。

---

- **A** What kind of music are you into? 你对什么音乐有兴趣？
- **B** I go for opera. 我喜欢歌剧。

---

- **A** Would you care for some oolong tea? 你要喝些乌龙茶吗？
- **B** Yes, that would be nice. 好的。那太好了。

---

- **A** Do you like this song? 你喜欢这首歌吗？
- **B** Yes, it started to grow on me. 是的，我越来越喜欢了。

---

- **A** Do you fancy going to a movie this Saturday?
  你这周六想不想去看电影？
- **B** No. I have an appointment with my dentist.
  不行，我已经约好要去看牙医了。

---

- **A** What are you up to recently? 最近在忙什么？
- **B** I'm addicted to photography. 我迷上摄影了。

Part 3 美国人聊天都说这些话

(相关会话群组记忆) 表达"不喜欢、不想要、讨厌"

20-05

★ **I don't like it.** ⌒任何情况皆适用 ……… 我不喜欢。
★ **I don't like it at all.** ……………… 我一点也不喜欢。
★ **I don't like ice cream.** ……………… 我不喜欢冰激凌。
★ **I don't like football.** ………………… 我不喜欢美式足球。
★ **I don't like to do housework.** …… 我不喜欢做家务。
★ **I don't like watching TV.** ………… 我不喜欢看电视。
★ **I hate it.** ⌒程度大于不喜欢 ……………… 我讨厌它。
★ **I hate singing.** ………………………… 我讨厌唱歌。
★ **I hate to get up early.** ……………… 我讨厌早起。
★ **I hate myself for making a mistake.**
   ……………………………………… 我痛恨自己犯了个错。
★ **I dislike vegetables.** ⌒较正式 …… 我不喜欢蔬菜。
★ **I dislike him.** ………………………… 我不喜欢他。
★ **I dislike working overtime.** ……… 我不喜欢加班。
★ **I have a distaste for fast food.** … 我不爱吃速食。
   ⌒distaste 表示"厌恶"
★ **I don't want to go to school.** …… 我不想上学。
★ **I don't want you to leave me.** … 我不想要你离开我。
★ **I don't want your money.** ………… 我不要你的钱。
★ **I don't love you anymore.** ………… 我不再爱你了。
★ **I despise irresponsible people.**
   ⌒despise 表示"看不起" ……………… 我鄙视不负责任的人。
★ **I'm not fond of skiing.** …………… 我不喜欢滑雪。
★ **I'm not keen on playing chess.** … 我不爱下棋。
★ **I detest arrogant people.** ………… 我厌恶自大的人。

★ **I detest washing dishes.** 我痛恨洗碗。
★ **I loathe your attitude.** 我厌恶你的态度。
★ **I loathe telling a lie.** 我厌恶说谎。
  ↳ loathe 表示"讨厌、厌恶"
★ **Most people abhor violence.**
  ↳ abhor 表示"憎恶、痛恨" 大部分的人痛恨暴力。

(20-06)

★ I have a (great) dislike for / of snakes.
  我（非常）不喜欢蛇。
★ He took a (strong) dislike to me. 他（非常）不喜欢我。
★ I would rather not tell you my secret.
  我宁愿不告诉你我的秘密。
★ I'm not interested in it. 我对此不感兴趣。
★ I'm not satisfied. 我不满意。
★ I don't feel like eating. 我不想吃。
★ I don't care for it. 我不喜欢。
★ This is disgusting. 这真恶心。
★ I can't stand it! 我受不了了！
★ I can't put up with him. 我无法忍受他。
★ I can't bear / endure it anymore. 我再也不能忍受了。
  ↳ bear、endure 表示"忍受"的意思
★ I've had it. / I've had enough. 我受够了。
★ It's enough. / That's enough. 够了。
★ That is not my style. 那不是我的风格。
★ It's boring. 这真无聊。
★ This movie sucks! 这部电影很烂！
  ↳ suck 表示"很烂"
★ I never eat Japanese food. 我从不吃日本料理。

- ★ Roger is not my type. ……………………… 罗杰不是我喜欢的类型。
- ★ Golf is not my (kind of) thing. ……………… 我不喜欢高尔夫球运动。
- ★ I don't think much of this new restaurant. …… 我不怎么喜欢这家新餐厅。
  - think much of 表示"看重"
- ★ I'm not a fan of social media. ………………… 我不喜欢社交媒体。
- ★ This show is not to my taste / liking. …………… 这场表演我不喜欢。
- ★ We object to this decision. …………………… 我们反对这个决定。
  - object to 表示"反对"
- ★ They view my opinions with disfavor. ………… 他们不赞成我的意见。
- ★ He was averse to helping me. ………………… 他不愿意帮助我。
  - averse 表示"不愿意的"
- ★ I have an aversion to cheese. ………………… 我对奶酪很反感。
- ★ I abominate school bullies. …………………… 我痛恨校园横行霸道者。
- ★ French cuisine doesn't appeal to me. …………… 法国菜并不吸引我。
- ★ She has no stomach for ballet. ………………… 她对芭蕾没兴趣。
  - have no stomach for sth. 表示"对……没兴趣、没胃口"
- ★ We took a dim view to this solution. ……… 我们不赞成这项解决方案。
- ★ Why do you have a down on me? ……………… 你为什么不喜欢我?
  - have a down on 表示"讨厌"
- ★ Musicals just leave me cold. ……………… 音乐剧就是提不起我的兴趣。
- ★ I'm reluctant to lend him money. ……………… 我不愿意借他钱。
  - reluctant 表示"不情愿的"
- ★ He is hostile to me. …………………………… 他对我有敌意。
- ★ I was repelled by the smell of vomit. ………… 呕吐的味道令我反感。
  - repel 表示"使反感"; vomit 表示"呕吐"
- ★ I was disinclined to clean my room. ……………… 我不想打扫房间。
  - disinclined 表示"不愿的"
- ★ He shrank from facing the challenge. ………… 他不愿面对挑战。
- ★ He scorned to accept my apology. …………… 他拒绝接受我的道歉。
- ★ She looked at me with repulsion. ……………… 她厌恶地看着我。
  - repulsion 表示"反感"

### 听美国人聊天

**A** I'm a vegetarian. Are you a vegetarian, too?
我吃素,你也吃素吗?

**B** No. I don't like vegetables. 不,我不喜欢蔬菜。

---

**A** How about watching the football game tonight?
今天晚上看美式足球赛如何?

**B** Oh, no, football is not my thing. 噢,不了,我不喜欢美式足球。

---

**A** Do you want to go to the night market? 你想去逛夜市吗?

**B** No. I'm not interested in it. 不,我没兴趣。

---

**A** How do you like Japanese food? 你觉得日本料理如何?

**B** Well, I don't really like it. 嗯,我不怎么喜欢。

---

**A** It's been raining for a week. 雨已经下了一个星期了。

**B** I hate this humid weather. I hope it clears up tomorrow.
我讨厌这种潮湿的天气,希望明天可以放晴。 → clear up 表示"放晴"

---

**A** I made some dumplings. Would you like to try some?
我包了一些水饺,你要不要吃一些?

**B** No, thanks. I have no stomach for that. 不,谢谢。我没胃口。

---

**A** How was the movie? 电影怎么样?

**B** It was boring. I didn't like it at all. 很无聊,我一点儿也不喜欢。

---

**A** Have you ever tried snake meat? 你吃过蛇肉吗?

**B** That sounds disgusting! 听起来好恶心!

---

**A** What kind of sport do you dislike? 你不喜欢哪种运动?

**B** I dislike ice hockey. 我不喜欢冰上曲棍球。

Part 3 美国人聊天都说这些话

英语的逻辑——30天学会美国人的英语逻辑

(美国人还会这样说) 其他与表达"好恶"相关的惯用语

## 1. Each has his likes and dislikes. 人各有喜好。

这句的字面意思是"每个人都有自己喜欢与不喜欢的事物",也就是"各有好恶""人各有喜好"的意思。

- Each has his likes and dislikes, so please respect me.

  人各有喜好,所以请尊重我。

## 2. Each follows his own bent. 人各有所好。

follow 是"追随",bent 是"天赋、天生的喜好"的意思。全句字面意思是"每个人追随自己的天赋",引申为"人各有所好"的意思。

- Each follows his own bent. I believe I will achieve my ambition.

  人各有所好,我相信我将能够实现我的抱负。

## 3. Tastes differ. 人各有所好。

taste 是"口味"的意思,differ 是"不同"的意思。这句字面上的意思是"每个人喜欢的口味有所不同",引申为"人各有所好"的意思。

- Tastes differ. I like Italian cuisine and my father likes Chinese food.

  人各有所好,我喜欢意大利菜而我父亲喜欢中国食物。

# Lesson 21  Under the Weather

## 身体不舒服

中文"**身体不舒服**",英语要如何表达呢?

就是"**under the weather**"。weather 是"天气"。"**under the weather**"字面解释是"在天气之下"。但是这个短语的意思跟天气状况并无直接关联,而是用来表示"身体不舒服""身体不适""生病"。所以,当你觉得身体不舒服时,可用"**under the weather**"来表达。

- I caught a cold. I felt under the weather.
  我感冒了,觉得身体不舒服。
  catch a cold 表示"感冒"

- I was a little bit under the weather. I think I need to see a doctor.
  我身体有点不舒服,我想我需要去看医生。

- I didn't go to school because I was under the weather.
  我没有去上学,因为我身体不舒服。

- You look under the weather. What's wrong with you?
  你看起来不太舒服,你怎么了?

- I couldn't make it to the meeting because I felt under the weather today.
  我没办法赶上会议,因为我今天身体不舒服。

**(相关会话群组记忆)** 表达"身体不舒服、不健康、生病"

21-02

- ★ I don't feel good. ……………………………… 我觉得不舒服。
- ★ I am sick. / I feel sick. ………………………… 我生病了。
- ★ I feel bad. ……………………………………… 我觉得不舒服。
- ★ I'm not well. …………………………………… 我不舒服。
- ★ I don't feel well. / I'm not feeling well.
  ……………………………………………………… 我觉得不舒服。
- ★ You don't look well. …………………………… 你看起来不太舒服。
- ★ I was feeling unwell. ………………………… 我觉得不舒服。
- ★ I am ill. / I feel ill. ……………………………… 我生病了。
- ★ I was / fell sick with the flu. …… 我患有流行性感冒。
- ★ I feel tired. ……………………………………… 我觉得累。
- ★ I felt fatigued. ………………………………… 我感到疲劳。
- ★ I was drained. ………………………………… 我觉得筋疲力尽。
- ★ I am run-down. ………………………………… 我感到筋疲力尽。
- ★ I'm feeling awful. ……………………………… 我觉得身体不舒服。
- ★ He was in bad shape. ………………………… 他健康状况不好。
  - ↪ in bad shape 表示"健康状况不好"
- ★ He is in poor health. ………………………… 他身体欠佳。
- ★ I don't feel myself today. …………………… 我今天觉得不舒服。
- ★ I feel a bit rough. ……………………………… 我觉得有点不舒服。
  - ↪ rough 表示"身体不适的"
- ★ I'm feeling queer. ……………………………… 我感到不舒服。
- ★ I feel poorly. …………………………………… 我觉得身体不舒服。
- ★ I feel under par. / I feel below par.
  - ↪ under par 表示"不舒服的" ……………… 我觉得不舒服。

★ I didn't sleep well. —— 我睡不好。
★ I have trouble sleeping. —— 我晚上睡不好觉。
★ I caught a cold. / I had a cold. —— 我感冒了。
★ I feel chilly. —— 我觉得很冷。
★ I was running a temperature. / I've got a temperature. —— 我在发烧。
★ I ran a fever. / I had a fever. —— 我发烧了。
★ I was feverish. ᵒ⁺feverish 表示"发烧的" —— 我发烧了。
★ I had a headache. —— 我头痛。
★ I had a bad headache. —— 我头很痛。
★ I had a splitting headache. —— 我头痛欲裂。
　ᵒ⁺splitting 表示"剧烈的"
★ My head is aching. / My head aches. —— 我头很痛。
★ My head hurts. —— 我头痛。
★ My head was pounding. —— 我头痛。
★ I have a migraine. —— 我有偏头痛。
★ I feel dizzy. —— 我觉得头晕。
★ I feel faint. ᵒ⁺faint、dizzy 表示"头晕的" —— 我觉得头晕。
★ I felt light-headed. —— 我觉得头晕。
★ My head is spinning. ᵒ⁺spin 表示"头晕" —— 我头很晕。
★ I have sore eyes. ᵒ⁺sore 表示"疼痛发炎的" —— 我眼睛痛。
★ I have itchy eyes. ᵒ⁺itchy 表示"痒的" —— 我眼睛很痒。
★ I have itchy skin. —— 我皮肤很痒。
★ I have a stuffy nose. —— 我鼻塞。
★ My nose is stuffed up. —— 我鼻塞。
★ I have a runny nose. —— 我流鼻涕。
★ My nose is running. —— 我流鼻涕了。
★ I've been sneezing all day. —— 我整天都在打喷嚏。
　ᵒ⁺sneeze 表示"打喷嚏"

- ★ She was on the sick-list. 她因病缺勤。
- ★ My thumb was hurt. 我的大拇指受伤了。
- ★ I cut my ring finger. 我割伤了无名指。
- ★ The suspect was wounded. **wound** 表示"使受伤" 嫌犯受伤了。
- ★ I have hay fever. **hay fever** 表示"花粉症" 我有花粉症。
- ★ I have a skin allergy. **allergy** 表示"过敏" 我皮肤过敏。
- ★ She is allergic to shrimp. 她对虾过敏。
- ★ Some people are allergic to gluten. 有些人对麸质过敏。
  **allergic** 表示"过敏的";**gluten** 表示"麸质、面筋"
- ★ Smoking is unhealthy for everyone. 抽烟对每个人都是不健康的。
- ★ He is a sickly old man. 他是一位多病的老人。
  **sickly** 表示"多病的"
- ★ He has suffered from knee pain. 他饱受膝盖疼痛之苦。
  **suffer from** 表示"患某种病"
- ★ He's been taking care of his ailing mother.
  **ailing** 表示"生病的" 他一直在照顾他生病的母亲。
- ★ She was laid up with fever. 她因发烧卧病在床。
  **laid up** 表示"卧病在床的";**laid up with...** 表示"因……卧病在床"
- ★ He broke his leg when falling down the stairs.
  他跌下楼梯时摔断了腿。
- ★ I have a pain in my chest. 我胸部很痛。
- ★ I have an ache in my lower abdomen. 我下腹部很痛。
  **abdomen** 表示"腹部"
- ★ Allen has been suffering from insomnia for a long time.
  **insomnia** 表示"失眠" 艾伦长期以来都受失眠折磨。
- ★ Jim suddenly blacked out after exercise. 吉姆运动后突然昏倒。
  **black out** 表示"昏倒"
- ★ Phillip suffered a concussion after a car accident.
  **concussion** 表示"脑震荡" 菲利浦在车祸之后脑震荡。

**听美国人聊天**

A What's wrong with you? 你怎么了？
B I'm not feeling well. 我觉得不舒服。

A You don't look well. Are you OK?
你看起来不是很好。你还好吗？
B I've come down with a fever. 我发烧了。

A I caught a cold. I have a runny nose and a sore throat.
我感冒了，流鼻涕又喉咙痛。
B That's too bad. I hope you get better soon.
太糟了，希望你赶快好起来。

A You look pale. What happened?
你看起来脸色苍白。怎么了？
B I ate too much and I have a stomachache.
我吃太多了，胃很痛。

A You look a bit off color. 你看起来脸色不佳。
B I have a bad headache. 我头很痛。

A Smoking is unhealthy. 抽烟不健康。
B I quit many years ago. 我很多年前就戒了。

A Are you all right? 你还好吗？
B I'm on my period. I have no appetite.
我例假来了，没有胃口。

A I've been coughing for three weeks. 我咳嗽三个星期了。
B You should see a doctor. 你应该去看医生。

(相关会话群组记忆) 表达"身体状况"

21-05

★ **I'm fine.** ← 任何情况皆适用 ·················· 我很好。
★ **I'm well now.** ································ 我现在病好了。
★ **I feel (much) better.** ······················· 我觉得好多了。
★ **I feel great. / I feel fine.** ················ 我很好。
★ **Very well.** ···································· 非常好。
★ **Not bad.** ······································ 还不错。
★ **I'm OK now.** ································· 我现在觉得很好。
★ **You look all right.** ·························· 你看起来还不错。
★ **You look fit.** ································· 你看起来很健康。

21-06

★ **Couldn't be better.** ························· 再好不过了。
★ **He is on the mend.** ·························· 他正在好转。
　↳ mend 表示"痊愈"；on the mend 表示"正在好转"
★ **He is fully recovered.** ····················· 他完全康复了。
★ **He is a robust young man.** ····· 他是一个身体强壮的年轻人。
　↳ robust 表示"强健的"
★ **He is in good health now.** ················ 他现在身体健康。
　↳ in good health 表示"身体健康"
★ **I have lower back pain.** ··················· 我腰痛。
★ **I had a severe pain in my lower back.** ··· 我腰部剧烈疼痛。
★ **He has been keeping in good condition.**
　↳ in good condition 表示"保持良好状态" ····· 他一直保持身体健康。
★ **I feel achy all over.** ························ 我浑身疼痛。
★ **I hope you are safe and sound.** ········· 希望你平安健康。
　↳ safe and sound 表示"平安无恙"

★ My left hand was twisted. ……………………… 我左手扭伤了。
  ↳ twist 表示"扭伤"
★ My left elbow joint hurt. ……………………… 我左手肘关节疼痛。
  ↳ elbow 表示"手肘";joint 表示"关节"
★ My lower back was strained. …………………… 我腰部拉伤。
  ↳ lower back 表示"下背部、腰部";strain 表示"拉伤"
★ My foot is swollen. ……………………………… 我的脚肿胀了。
★ He has high blood pressure. ………………… 他有高血压。

(21-07)

★ He is an able-bodied man. …………………… 他身体很健壮。
  ↳ able-bodied 表示"体格强壮的"
★ He is fit as a fiddle. …………………………… 他非常健康。
  ↳ fiddle 表示"小提琴";fit as a fiddle 表示"非常健康"
★ I'm glad to hear that David is still alive and kicking.
  ……………………………… 很高兴知道大卫现在还是生龙活虎的。
★ I feel fighting fit after exercise. ……………… 我运动后觉得精力充沛。
  ↳ fighting fit 表示"身体很强健"
★ I'm in the pink. ………………………………… 我身体很健康。
  ↳ in the pink 表示"身体健康"
★ You look in fine fettle. ………………………… 你看起来身体很健康。
  ↳ fettle 表示"身体状况";in fine fettle 表示"身体健康"
★ I feel fresh after a shower. …………………… 我淋浴后觉得精力充沛。
★ He is strong and never gets sick. …………… 他身体强壮,从未生过病。
★ You look the picture of health. ……………… 你看起来很健康。
★ I am right as rain after a few days of rest.
  ……………………………… 经过几天休息,我觉得好多了。
★ My husband is strong as an ox. ……………… 我丈夫壮得像头牛。
★ I'm feeling up to snuff. ………………………… 我觉得自己身体健康。
  ↳ up to snuff 表示"健康正常的"
★ My grandmother is still very hale and hearty. ·· 我祖母身体还很硬朗。

Part 3 美国人聊天都说这些话

**听美国人聊天**

**A** How is Sam? Is he getting any better?
萨姆怎么样？他好一些了吗？
**B** He is on the mend. 他正在好转当中。

---

**A** Are you feeling all right? 你现在觉得还好吗？
**B** Thank you. I feel much better now. 谢谢你，我现在觉得好多了。

---

**A** You look fit as a fiddle. 你身体看起来很健康。
**B** I've been working out for half a year. 我健身半年了。

---

**A** I heard that you were ill. 我听说你生病了。
**B** Yes, but I'm fully recovered. I feel like a new person now.
是的，但是我完全康复了，我现在感觉焕然一新。

---

**A** What's your favorite sport? 你最喜欢什么运动？
**B** Jogging. I do it every day. It makes me feel healthy.
慢跑。我每天慢跑，这让我觉得很健康。

---

**A** You look so energetic! How do you keep yourself in good health? 你看起来真有活力！你是如何保持健康的？
**B** Well, I don't smoke and I never drink.
嗯，我不抽烟也从不喝酒。

---

**A** I can't go to class today. 我今天不能去上课。
**B** Why not? 为什么不能去？
**A** I've got a temperature. 我在发烧。

---

**A** You look tired today. What's the matter?
你今天看起来很累。怎么了？
**B** I had trouble sleeping last night. 我昨晚睡不着觉。

(美国人还会这样说) **其他与表达"健康"相关的惯用语**

## 1. have one foot in the grave 一只脚已踏进坟墓

grave 是"坟墓"的意思。这句的字面意思是"一只脚已踏进坟墓",引申为"活不久了""行将就木""棺材都进了一半了"的意思。

- Mr. Johnson is old and ill. He has one foot in the grave.

  约翰逊先生年老多病,已经一只脚踏在坟墓里了。

## 2. just what the doctor ordered 正是我所需要的

order 是"医生嘱咐"的意思,这句的字面意思是"正是医生所嘱咐的""正是医生开的药方"。医生开的药方是为了治疗疾病,因此可引申为"对症下药""正是某人所需要的东西"。

- After working all day, a hearty meal is just what the doctor ordered.

  工作一整天后,一顿丰盛的大餐正是我所需要的。

## 3. a bitter pill to swallow 不得不接受的事实

bitter 表示"苦的",pill 是"药丸"的意思,swallow 是"吞下"的意思。全句字面意思是"必须吞下的苦药丸",引申为"不得不做的苦事""不得不接受的事实"。

- Losing the game for me is a bitter pill to swallow.

  对我而言,输掉比赛是一个不得不接受的事实。

## Lesson 22  It Bores Me to Death

# 无聊透顶

中文"无聊透顶",英语要如何表达呢?

就是"It bores me to death"。bore 是"使无聊、使厌烦"的意思。to death 是"极度、极其、非常"的意思。全句字面上的解释是"这让我无聊死了""这让我感到无聊至极"。这是比较夸张的说法,用来形容某件事无聊到令你想死。因此,当某件事令你感到极其乏味、无聊至极、无聊透顶时,即可使用"It bores me to death"来表达。

- This movie bores me to death.
  这部电影无聊透顶。

- The tedious speech bored us to death.
  冗长的演讲让我们感到乏味至极。
  ↳ tedious 表示"冗长乏味的"

- I am bored to death. I don't know what to do.
  我好无聊,不知道要做什么。

- The daily routines really bore me to death.
  日常例行公事实在令我感到无聊透顶。
  ↳ routine 表示"例行公事"

- My job bores me to death. I need a vacation.
  我的工作乏味至极,我需要度个假。

**相关会话群组记忆** 表达"觉得很无聊、某事很无聊"

★ **I am bored. / I feel bored.** 🖝任何情况皆适用
我觉得很无聊。

★ **It's so boring.** 这好无聊。

★ **What a bore!** 这真是无聊!

★ **It's such a bore!** 这真是太无聊了!

★ **It's a bore to me.** 这对我来说很无聊。
🖝 bore 在这里是名词,表示"无聊的事"

★ **How boring! / How tedious!** 多无聊啊!

★ **This performance is tedious.**
这场表演很冗长乏味。

★ **This book is dull.** 这本书很沉闷。
🖝 dull 表示"乏味的、单调的"

★ **This story is dreary.** 这个故事很枯燥。

★ **The novel is so uninspired.** 这本小说很没创意。
🖝 uninspired 表示"缺乏创意的"

★ **This joke is so lame.** 这个笑话很无趣。

★ **You are so lame.** 你好无趣。

★ **I'm getting stale at work.** 我对工作越来越厌倦。
🖝 stale 表示"厌倦的"

★ **This conversation is tiresome.** 这对话很沉闷。
🖝 tiresome 表示"沉闷的"

★ **My life is monotonous.** 我的生活很单调。
🖝 monotonous 表示"单调乏味的"

★ **It's dull.** 这很乏味。

★ **I feel so flat.** 我觉得好无聊。

★ **This play is so dry.** 这部戏剧好枯燥乏味。

★ **Today's game was unexciting.**
今天的比赛很无聊。

★ **Your ideas sound trite.** 你的意见听起来很老套。
  ↪ trite 表示"陈腐的"

★ **This is an arid course.** 这是一门枯燥的课程。
  ↪ arid 除了表示"不毛的、贫瘠的",还可表示"枯燥的"

★ **Her dance is lifeless.** 她的舞蹈很呆板。

★ **This is a lackluster piano performance.**
  ↪ lackluster 表示"无聊、无趣的" 这是一场无聊的钢琴表演。

★ **It is a vapid suggestion.** 这是个无趣的提议。

---

(22-03)

★ This class is boring. 这堂课很无聊。
★ The new products are uninspiring. 新产品引不起兴趣。
  ↪ uninspiring 表示"引不起兴趣的"
★ It's boring to go shopping. 去逛街很无聊。
★ I'm bored stiff. 我无聊透了。
★ This is not so interesting. 这不是很有趣。
★ I'm not interested in it. 我对此不感兴趣。
★ He is an uninteresting man. 他是一个无趣的人。
★ This article is very uninteresting. 这篇文章非常无趣。
★ I found it uninteresting. 我觉得这很无聊。
★ The TV news is boring. 电视新闻很无聊。
★ The show bored me stiff. 这场表演快把我无聊死了。
  ↪ bore sb. stiff 表示"令某人觉得无聊透顶"
★ I don't find it interesting at all. 我一点也不觉得这有趣。
★ I'm bored out of my mind. 我觉得无聊极了。
★ What a drag! 好无聊!

★ The party was a drag. ……………………… 派对好无聊。
★ Mrs. Anderson is such a drag. ·· 安德森太太是个无趣的人。
  ↪ drag 表示"无聊的人或事"
★ Tonight's concert was a yawn. ……… 今晚的音乐会很乏味。
★ My daily work is so routine. ………… 我的日常工作很乏味。
  ↪ routine 表示"普通的、乏味的"
★ My college life was humdrum. ……… 我的大学生活好无聊。
  ↪ humdrum 表示"无聊的、乏味的"
★ It was a ho-hum kind of day. ………… 今天真是无聊的一天。
★ I'm tired of your wearisome complaints.
  ………………………………………………… 我对你无聊的抱怨感到厌倦。
★ Mr. Rochester is an insipid old man.
  ↪ insipid 表示"无趣的" ………… 罗切斯特先生是一个无趣的老人。

★ It bores me to tears. …………… 这让我无聊到想哭。/ 这真是无聊至极。
★ The meeting bored me. ……………………………… 会议令我感到无聊。
★ It's a bore to stay home all day. ………………… 整天待在家很无聊。
★ I can't tolerate the boredom of waiting. ……… 我无法忍受等待的无聊。
  ↪ boredom 表示"无聊"
★ This lecture is as dry as dust. …………………………… 这次讲座非常乏味。
  ↪ as dry as dust 表示"非常乏味的"
★ It leaves me cold. ………………………………………… 这无法提起我的兴趣。
★ The football games just leave me cold. … 我对美式足球赛就是提不起劲。
  ↪ leave sb. cold 表示"无法引起某人兴趣"
★ She is such a wet blanket. ……………………… 她真是一个扫兴的人。
★ Don't be a wet blanket! ……………………………………… 别让人扫兴！
★ You just threw a wet blanket on my plan. ……… 你对我的计划泼冷水。
  ↪ throw a wet blanket on... 表示"对……泼冷水、使扫兴"
★ Don't rain on my parade. ……………………… 别给我浇冷水。/ 别扫兴。
★ Most TV programs are mind-numbing.
  ………………………………………… 大部分电视节目都无聊到令人头脑麻木。

## 听美国人聊天

**A** I'm tired of my daily work. 我对每天的工作感到厌烦。
**B** Maybe you need a vacation. 也许你需要度个假。

---

**A** How was the movie? 电影好看吗？
**B** The movie put me to sleep. It was boring and dull.
我看到睡着，很无聊沉闷。 → put me to sleep 表示"某事无聊到让我睡着了"

---

**A** It's so boring. I have nothing to do. 好无聊，我无事可做。
**B** Well, you can buy me a drink. 噢，你可以请我喝一杯。

---

**A** I'm getting into golf recently. Do you like it, too?
我最近开始迷上高尔夫球，你也喜欢吗？ → get into... 表示"开始对……有兴趣"
**B** No. Golf just leaves me cold.
不喜欢，我对高尔夫球就是提不起劲。

---

**A** How was your day today? 你今天过得怎么样？
**B** It was a ho-hum kind of day. Nothing happened at all.
今天真是无聊的一天，什么事都没发生。

---

**A** Did you watch the semifinal of the Australian Open yesterday? 你昨天看澳大利亚网球公开赛的半决赛了吗？
→ semifinal 表示"半决赛"
**B** Yes, and the game was not as exciting as I expected.
看了，比赛并没有我期待的那么刺激。

---

**A** I'm thinking about inviting Jasmine to my birthday party.
我正在考虑邀请杰斯敏参加我的生日派对。
**B** Are you sure? Because she is such a wet blanket!
你确定吗？她是个很扫兴的人！

**相关会话群组记忆** 表达"觉得很有趣;人、事、物很吸引人"

- ★ **It's interesting.** ⟵任何情况皆适用 ……… 这真有趣。
- ★ **It's funny.** ……………………………………… 这真有趣。
- ★ **It's meaningful.** …………………………… 这很有意义。
- ★ **It's exciting.** ………………………………… 真是太刺激了。
- ★ **I'm so excited! / I feel so excited!** ……… 我好兴奋!
- ★ **Sounds good / great / fantastic.**
  ………………………………… 听起来很好 / 很棒 / 很赞。

- ★ It's an exciting game. ……………… 这是一场令人振奋的比赛。
- ★ I found it interesting. …………………………… 我觉得这很有趣。
- ★ I was thrilled to meet you! …………………… 遇到你我很激动!
  ⟵ thrilled 表示"激动的、开心的"
- ★ This is an interesting place. ………… 这是个很好玩的地方。
- ★ The song you wrote is so moving. ……… 你写的歌很动人。
- ★ It's fun to jump rope. ……………………………… 跳绳很好玩。
- ★ We had a fun time today at the beach.
  …………………………………… 我们今天在海边玩得很开心。
- ★ How amusing! …………………………………………… 真有趣!
- ★ These photos are amusing. ………………… 这些照片很有趣。
- ★ We had an enjoyable picnic today.
  ………………………………………… 今天我们有愉快的野餐。
- ★ What a pleasing sight it is! ……… 这是多么令人愉快的景色!
  ⟵ pleasing 表示"令人愉快的"
- ★ Asian cuisine is so appealing. ………… 亚洲菜非常吸引人。
- ★ I found him very attractive. ………… 我觉得他很有吸引力。

★ This is an engaging city. ………… 这是一个迷人的城市。
★ She is such an engaging girl. …… 她是这么一个可爱的女孩。
★ She gave me an alluring look. …… 她给我一个迷人的眼神。
★ His smile is so captivating. ………… 他的笑容非常有魅力。
　↪ captivating 表示"有魅力的"
★ These fruits look so inviting. ……… 这些水果看起来很好吃。
★ She is such an enchanting woman.
　↪ enchanting 表示"迷人的" ………… 她是一位如此迷人的女性。
★ I have an unusual name. ………… 我有一个很奇特的名字。
★ This website is very entertaining. … 这个网站很有娱乐性。
★ Most adventure novels are absorbing.
　……………………………………… 大部分的冒险小说都很引人入胜。
★ These fairy tales are pretty gripping.
　↪ gripping 表示"扣人心弦的"……… 这些童话故事相当扣人心弦。
★ Your plan sounds very enticing. … 你的计划听起来很诱人。
★ I had an exhilarating experience of bungee jumping.
　……………………………………… 我有一次非常令人振奋的蹦极经验。

22-07

★ That aroused my curiosity. ……………………… 那激起了我的好奇心。
　↪ arouse 表示"唤起"
★ I was on the edge of my seat. ………………………… 我很紧张兴奋。
★ I was carried away by this song. ……………… 这首歌令我激动不已。
　↪ be / get carried away 表示"激动、入迷"
★ We whooped it up at the party. …………………… 我们在派对上狂欢。
★ I was pumped for the boxing match yesterday.
　……………………………………………… 昨天的拳击比赛让我很振奋。
★ The speech pumped us up. ………………… 这场演讲令我们感到很振奋。
★ I'm pumped up about this trip. …………… 我对这次旅游感到很兴奋。
　↪ pump sb. up 表示"使……振奋，兴奋"
★ The whole game was a nail-biter. ………… 整场比赛都令人非常紧张。

> **听美国人聊天**

**A** I'm planning to go rock climbing with my friends.
我打算跟我朋友一起去攀岩。
**B** Sounds exciting. 听起来很刺激。

---

**A** I'm so excited about my wedding. 我对我的婚礼感到好兴奋。
**B** It's going to be so much fun. 一定会很好玩。

---

**A** What type of food do you like? 你喜欢哪一种食物?
**B** I like Korean food. It's very appealing to me.
我喜欢韩国料理。它非常吸引我。

---

**A** I made a vanilla cake by myself for the first time yesterday. 昨天我第一次自己做香草蛋糕。
**B** That's interesting! 真是有趣!

---

**A** I was stoked that I got a promotion. 我升迁了,我好兴奋。
**B** Congratulations! That's great! 恭喜!真是太棒了!

---

**A** This speech really pumped me up.
这场演讲令我感到十分振奋。
**B** It's very inspiring. I was moved, too.
非常激励人心,我也非常感动。

---

**A** How do you like my new book? 你觉得我的新书如何?
**B** Overall the book is great and the story is very absorbing. 整体上这本书很好,而且故事很引人入胜。

---

**A** Hey, why don't we go backpacking?
嘿,我们何不去自助旅行?
**B** Your plan sounds very enticing. 你的计划听起来很诱人。

(美国人还会这样说) **其他与表达"无聊、乏味"相关的惯用语**

## 1. a stick in the mud 老古董

stick 是"树枝"的意思，mud 是"泥沼"的意思。这句字面上的意思是"陷入泥沼的树枝"，用来比喻一个人古板、保守又墨守成规，相当无聊乏味。

- I can't believe he is such a stick in the mud. He seems open-minded.
  
  我不敢相信他这么老古董，他看起来相当开明。

## 2. as dull as ditchwater (dishwater) 沉闷无聊

dull 是"沉闷"的意思，ditchwater 是"沟中死水"的意思。这句字面上的意思是"如同沟中死水一样沉闷"，用来比喻极度无聊沉闷。另外，ditchwater 也可用 dishwater（洗碗水）替代。

- Your presentation was as dull as ditchwater. I even fell asleep.
  
  你的报告极度沉闷无聊，我甚至睡着了。

## 3. as interesting as watching paint dry 无聊

paint 是"油漆"的意思。这句字面上的意思是"如同观看油漆干掉一样有趣"，用来比喻相当枯燥、乏味。

- Modern dance is too abstract for me to understand. Watching modern dance is as interesting as watching paint dry.
  
  现代舞对我来说太抽象，无法理解。因此观看现代舞相当无聊。

# Lesson 23 Calm Down

## 冷静下来

中文"冷静下来",英语要如何表达呢?

就是"calm down"。calm 是"冷静"的意思。calm down 就是"冷静下来、镇定下来""使冷静、使镇定"的意思。当有人很激动或是很生气,而你想要叫他们冷静下来时,即可使用"calm down"这个短语。

- Why are you so angry? Just calm down!
  你为什么这么生气?冷静下来!

- Why don't you calm down and have a cup of tea?
  你为什么不冷静下来并且喝杯茶?

- I need to calm down and relax.
  我需要冷静并且放松。

- I need some time to calm down and think it over.
  我需要一些时间冷静下来并仔细思考。

- Please calm down before you do something stupid.
  在你做出蠢事之前,请冷静下来。

- I won't talk to you unless you calm down.
  除非你冷静下来,否则我不会跟你说话。

- Louise finally calmed down and apologized to me.
  路易丝最终冷静下来向我道歉了。

**相关会话群组记忆** 表达"冷静下来、镇定、放松、休息一下"

- ★ **Keep calm. / Stay calm.** —— 保持冷静。
- ★ **Be cool.** —— 冷静一点。
- ★ **Cool it down.** ✎俚语 —— 冷静下来。
- ★ **Cool down.** —— 冷静。/ 镇定。
- ★ **Cool off.** —— 冷静。/ 镇静。
- ★ **Cool out.** —— 冷静。/ 放松。
- ★ **Keep your cool. / Remain cool. / Stay cool.**
   —— 保持冷静。
- ★ **Chill. / Chill out.** —— 冷静下来。
- ★ **Just relax.** —— 放松一点。
- ★ **I feel relaxed.** —— 我觉得放松。
- ★ **Control yourself.** —— 克制自己。
- ★ **Contain yourself.** —— 克制自己。
- ★ **Take it easy.** —— 别生气。/ 放轻松。/ 别紧张。/ 别激动。
- ★ **Take a break.** —— 休息一下。
- ★ **Take a rest.** —— 休息一下。
- ★ **Take ten.** —— 休息一会儿。
- ★ **Take your time.** —— 慢慢来。/ 别着急。
- ★ **Take a breather.** —— 休息一下。
- ★ **Collect yourself. / Collect your thoughts.**
   ✎ collect 表示"使镇静" —— 镇定下来。
- ★ **Compose yourself.** —— 镇定下来。
   ✎ compose 表示"使镇静"
- ★ **Ease off. / Ease up.** —— 放松。
- ★ **Just hang loose.** —— 保持镇定。
   ✎ hang loose 表示"镇定"

★ Don't have a cow. ……………………………… 别生气。
  ↳ cow 表示"母牛",这句是表示"别生气、别激动"
★ Don't sweat it. ↳俚语 ………………………………… 别紧张。
★ Wind down. …………………………………………… 放松一下。
★ Go easy on me. ↳较口语 ……… 对我宽容些。/ 别对我太苛刻。
★ I feel at ease. ………………………………………… 我觉得放松。
★ Simmer down. ………………………………………… 冷静下来。
★ Lighten up. …………………………………… 放轻松。/ 高兴一点。
★ You need to mellow out. ………………………… 你需要放松一点。
  ↳ mellow out 表示"放松一点"
★ Let yourself go. ……………………………………… 让自己放松。
★ Keep your shirt on. ……………………………………… 冷静点。
★ Don't panic. ↳panic 表示"恐慌" ……………………… 不要恐慌。
★ He is so together. …………………………………… 他是如此沉着。
★ Loosen up. Everything will be OK.
  …………………………………………… 放松一点,一切都会没事。
★ You can breathe easy. / You can rest easy.
  ………………………………………………… 你可以松一口气了。
★ I just sit around all day. ………………………… 我整天都无所事事。
  ↳ sit around 表示"闲坐无所事事"
★ I am able to keep my head in any situation.
  ……………………………………… 我在任何情况下都能够保持冷静。
★ You have to keep a clear head in the exam.
  ………………………………………… 你在考试时必须保持头脑清醒。
★ I have the presence of mind to deal with any problem.
  …………………………………………………… 我能够冷静处理任何问题。
★ She is so free and easy. ……………………… 她非常不拘小节。
★ She seems casual about everything.
  ………………………………………… 她似乎对所有事情都漫不经心。

- ★ I feel peaceful inside. ……………………………… 我内心觉得平静。
- ★ Please make yourself at home. ……………………… 请别拘束。
  - at home 表示"觉得自在"
- ★ Restrain yourself. …………………………………… 克制自己一下。
- ★ He is very self-controlled. ………………………… 他非常有自制力。
- ★ She looks self-possessed. ………………………… 她看起来很沉着。
  - self-possessed 表示"沉着、冷静"
- ★ You need to get hold of yourself. ……………… 你需要控制一下自己。
- ★ I tried to regain my composure. ………………… 我试图恢复镇静。
- ★ He always looks so composed. …………… 他看起来总是很冷静沉着。
  - composed 表示"沉着的、镇静的"
- ★ She is level-headed. / She has a level head. …………… 她很冷静。
- ★ You need to take a chill pill. …………………… 你需要冷静一下。
- ★ You can put your feet up. ……………………… 你可以坐着好好放松。
  - 字面上的意思是"把脚翘起来",表示"坐着放松"
- ★ Just let your hair down. ……………………… 放轻松。/ 尽情享受。
- ★ Keep your hair on. …………………………………… 保持冷静。
- ★ I feel laid-back. 俚语 …………………………………… 我觉得很放松。
- ★ Music can soothe me. ……………………………… 音乐可以让我感到平静。
- ★ Vivian is not fazed by anything at all.
  - faze 表示"使惊慌失措" ………… 薇薇安对任何事都不会惊慌失措。
- ★ I listen to music to unwind. …………………… 我听音乐放松心情。
  - unwind 表示"放松心情"
- ★ Jessica looks poised and confident. …… 杰西卡看起来冷静且有自信。
- ★ She is very coolheaded. ………………………… 她头脑很冷静。
- ★ He is a placid boy. ……………………………… 他是一个温和的男孩。
- ★ Austin seems unfazed by anything.
  - unfazed 表示"处变不惊的" ……… 奥斯汀似乎对任何事都处变不惊。
- ★ I tried to pacify my crying baby. ………… 我试图安抚正在哭泣的宝宝。
- ★ This is a tranquil place. ………………………… 这是一个平静的地方。
- ★ It's hard to remain imperturbable all the time.
  - imperturbable 表示"冷静的" ……………… 要一直保持冷静很不容易。

**听美国人聊天**

A  I can't believe my car was stolen! 真不敢相信我的车被偷了!
B  Calm down! Did you call the police? 冷静一点!你报警了吗?

A  I'm so nervous about my first date.
   我对于第一次约会感到很紧张。
B  Just relax. Everything will be fine. 放松一点,一切都会很好。

A  Welcome to my apartment. Please make yourself at home. 欢迎来到我的公寓,请不要拘束。
B  Thank you. 谢谢你。

A  I think I'm a bit pessimistic. Sometimes I just worry too much. 我想我有点悲观,有时候我就是会过于烦恼。
B  Lighten up! Look on the bright side. 放轻松!要保持乐观。
   → look on the bright side 表示"看事情的光明面、保持乐观态度"

A  I've been working all day and I'm so exhausted.
   我工作了一整天,现在好累。
B  You need to loosen up. 你需要放松一下。

A  I don't know why I always get angry with my husband.
   我不知道为什么我总是对我的老公很生气。
B  Take it easy. Don't be so serious. 放轻松,别这么严肃。

A  What do you do to relax? 你都做什么来放松自己?
B  I go to the gym three times a week. 我一星期去健身房三次。

A  Hurry up. We're late! 快点,我们迟到了!
B  Chill out! We have plenty of time. 放轻松,我们还有很多时间。

Part 3 美国人聊天都说这些话

(相关会话群组记忆) 表达"无法冷静、紧张、焦虑、害怕"

23-05

★ **I'm afraid of making a mistake.** …… 我害怕犯错。
★ **I'm afraid of the dark.** ………………… 我怕黑。
★ **I'm frightened of heights.** …………… 我有恐高症。
★ **I'm scared of eels.** ……………………… 我怕鳗鱼。
★ **I'm scared to death.** …………………… 我怕得要死。
★ **I'm terrified of cockroaches.** ……… 我怕蟑螂。
★ **I'm petrified of thunder.** …………… 我非常怕雷声。
★ **I'm so nervous.** ↙任何情况皆适用 …… 我好紧张。
★ **I'm so nervous about the job interview.**

………………………………… 我对于工作面试感到好紧张。

★ **I am nervy about flying.** …… 我对坐飞机感到紧张。

↙ nervy 表示"紧张不安的"

★ **I feel uneasy.** …………………………… 我觉得不安。
★ **I'm so anxious about the result of the test.**

………………………………… 我对于测验结果感到很焦虑。

★ **I'm a little on edge.** …………… 我有一点儿紧张。
★ **I'm edgy about it.** ………………… 我对此感到紧张。
★ **I am apprehensive of the outcome.**

………………………………………………… 我对结果很担心。

★ **I feel so jumpy.** ………………………… 我感到心惊肉跳。

↙ jumpy 表示"神经质的"

★ **The noise makes me jittery.** …… 噪声令我心烦意乱。
★ **He is too timid to try something new.**

↙ timid 表示"胆小的" ……… 他太胆小不敢尝试新事物。

★ **I tremble to think of it.** ……………… 我为此而担心。

★ Melody only has her boyfriend on her mind.
梅洛迪只挂念她的男朋友。
★ I fear for his health. 我担心他的健康。
　↳ fear for 表示"担心"
★ I'm in a sweat about the money. 我为钱的事焦急。
★ I am ill at ease. 我坐立不安。
★ I'm on pins and needles. 我如坐针毡。
★ I'm under the gun to finish the paper.
我赶报告很有压力。
★ I was a bundle of nerves before the speech.
我在演讲前非常紧张。

★ I have butterflies in my stomach. 我非常紧张。
★ I had cold feet before riding a roller coaster.
我在搭过山车前临阵退缩。
★ Ghost stories always give me the creeps.
鬼故事总是令我感到毛骨悚然。
★ This horror movie made my flesh creep. 这部恐怖片令我汗毛直竖。
★ It makes my blood freeze. 这令我不寒而栗。
★ Earthworms make my skin crawl. 蚯蚓令我全身起鸡皮疙瘩。
★ I've got goosebumps. / I've got goose pimples. 我起鸡皮疙瘩了。
★ This really gives me the heebie-jeebies.
　↳ heebie-jeebies 表示"神经紧张、焦虑" 这真的令我神经紧张。
★ I have ants in my pants. 我坐立不安。
　↳ 字面意思是"有蚂蚁在我的裤子里",表示"坐立不安"
★ I was shaking like a leaf. 我紧张到浑身发抖。
★ I broke out in a cold sweat. 我吓出一身冷汗。
★ I'm all hot and bothered. 我觉得心烦意乱。

**听美国人聊天**

A I'm so nervous about the job interview.
我对于面试感到很紧张。

B Don't worry. You'll be great. 别担心,你会表现得很好。

---

A I have butterflies in my stomach before the speech.
我在演讲前都会很紧张。

B Try to take a deep breath and relax. 试着深呼吸并且放松。

---

A I think I'm a little too timid to try something new.
我想我有点儿太胆小,以至于不敢尝试新事物。

B Maybe you're just afraid of making a mistake.
也许你只是害怕犯错。

---

A Why are you so tense now? 你现在怎么这么紧张?

B I guess I'm a little nervous about flying.
我想我对坐飞机有点儿紧张。

---

A I'm so anxious about how I did on the test.
我对于测验结果感到很焦虑。

B Don't worry. I'm sure you'll do fine.
别担心,我相信你会做得很好。

---

A Bella seemed distracted today. 贝拉今天看起来心烦意乱的。

→ distracted 表示"心烦意乱的、分神的"

B She only has her boyfriend on her mind.
她只挂念她的男朋友。

---

A I can't stand that noise. It makes me jittery.
我受不了那噪声。它令我神经紧张。

B You can wear earplugs. 你可以戴耳塞。

(美国人还会这样说) 其他与表达"冷静、放松"相关的惯用语

## 1. pull yourself together 冷静点

pull 是"拉"的意思,这句字面意思是"把自己拉回来"。表示把自己拉回来,以打起精神控制自己、恢复镇定的意思。

- Pull yourself together! There is still a lot of work to do.
  冷静点!还有很多事要做。

## 2. as cool as a cucumber 泰然自若

cool 是"冷静"的意思,cucumber 是"小黄瓜"的意思。这句字面上的意思是"如同小黄瓜一样冷静",用来比喻一个人非常冷静、泰然自若的样子。

- Curtis is as cool as a cucumber even in such a difficult situation.
  即使在这样一个困难的处境中,柯提斯依然泰然自若。

## 3. hold your horses 冷静点

hold 是"拉住"的意思。这句字面上的意思是"拉住你的马",用来比喻别急躁、冷静点。

- Hold your horses and let me explain myself.
  冷静点,让我解释一下。

# Lesson 24　As Easy As Pie

## 易如反掌

中文"易如反掌",英语要如何表达呢?

就是"as easy as pie"。pie 是"派、馅饼"的意思。全句字面意思是"如同派一样简单",形容某事情非常容易。因此,当你想要表达某件事"非常容易、简单""轻而易举""易如反掌""小事一桩"时,可使用"as easy as pie"这个短语。

- The exam is as easy as pie.
  这次考试非常简单。

- Math is as easy as pie for me.
  数学对我来说很简单。

- Learning to swim is as easy as pie.
  学游泳非常容易。

- This crossword puzzle is as easy as pie.
  这个填字游戏非常简单。

- Developing good habits is as easy as pie.
  养成好习惯是轻而易举的事。

- Making fried rice is as easy as pie.
  炒饭非常容易做。

- It's as easy as pie for me to save money.
  存钱对我而言非常容易。

(相关会话群组记忆) 表达"非常容易、轻而易举、小事一桩"

★ **As easy as ABC / 123 / anything / winking / falling off a log.** ……… 极其容易。
★ **It's so easy.** ……………………… 这很容易。
★ **It's not complicated.** ……………… 这并不复杂。
★ **This task is not burdensome.** 这个工作并不繁重。
　↳ burdensome 表示"繁重的"
★ **It's really simple.** ………………… 这很简单。
★ **It's not difficult.** ………………… 这不难。
★ **It's a piece of cake.** ……………… 这很简单。
★ **It's a cakewalk.** …………………… 这太容易了。
　↳ cakewalk 表示"很容易做的事"
★ **It's no big deal.** …………………… 这又没什么。
★ **It's child's play. / It's kid's stuff.**
　………………………………………… 这很容易。
★ **It's a snap.** ⌒较口语 …………… 易如反掌。
★ **It's a cinch.** ⌒俚语 ……………… 这简单得很。
★ **It's a no-brainer.** ………………… 这是很容易的事。
★ **It's a doddle.** ⌒较口语 ………… 这件事非常容易。
★ **It's a breeze.** ……………………… 这件事轻而易举。

★ No problem. ………………………………………… 没问题。
★ It's no bother. ……………………………… 一点儿也不麻烦。
★ No sweat. ……………………………… 不费力。/ 一点儿都不难。
★ There is nothing to it. ……………………… 这非常简单。

★ This will be easily done. ……………… 这件事很容易完成。
★ It's a sure thing. ……………………………… 当然可以。
★ This is a cushy job. ……………………… 这是一个轻松的工作。
  ↳ cushy 表示"容易的、轻松的"
★ Anyone can do it. ……………………………… 这谁都做得到。
★ Singing comes easily to me. ……………… 我生来就会唱歌。
  ↳ come easily 表示"易如反掌、生来就会"
★ This is the easiest thing in the world.
  …………………………………………………… 这是全世界最容易的事。
★ This is an easy book. ……………………… 这本书很简单。
★ This is a foolproof system. ……… 这是一个简单明了的系统。
  ↳ foolproof 表示"傻瓜也会了解的、不会出错的"
★ I did it without difficulty. ……………… 我轻易完成了这件事。
★ He accomplished the job with ease. ·· 他轻松完成了工作。
  ↳ with ease 表示"轻而易举地"
★ They won the game with no effort.
  …………………………………………………… 他们毫不费力赢得了比赛。
★ This is self-explanatory. ……………… 这是不证自明的。
★ This is a straightforward question. ·· 这是一个简单的问题。
  ↳ straightforward 表示"简单的、易懂的"
★ It's a clear example. ……………………… 这是个清楚的例子。
★ The gyms are accessible to the students.
  …………………………………………………… 学生都可使用体育馆。
★ He handily solved the problem. …… 他轻易地解决了问题。
  ↳ handily 表示"轻易地"
★ It's all downhill from here. ……………… 之后的都很容易。
★ The policy is low-hanging fruit. ……… 新政策很容易实现。
★ The factory is running smoothly. ……… 工厂运作顺利。
  ↳ smoothly 表示"顺利地"
★ The plan was carried out without a hitch.
  …………………………………………………… 计划顺利进行。

★ I had no trouble finishing the task. ……… 我很容易就完成这个任务。
★ I can understand this article without any trouble.
……………………………………………… 我可轻易了解这篇文章。
★ It's not rocket science. …………………………… 这不是什么难事。
  rocket science 表示"火箭科学",代表"高深的事"
★ Everything is plain-sailing. ……… 一切都一帆风顺。/ 一切都很顺利。
★ This is a pushover. …………………………… 这件事很容易完成。
  pushover 表示"容易做的事"
★ I took the soft / easy option. ………………… 我做了轻松的选择。
★ I always choose the line of least resistance.
……………………………………………… 我总是选择最省力的方法。
★ The math test is a walk in the park. ………… 这次数学测验很简单。
  a walk in the park 表示"容易的事"
★ Cooking is duck soup for me. ………………… 烹饪对我来说轻而易举。
★ This product is user-friendly. ……………… 这项产品非常容易使用。
  -friendly 表示"对……友善的"
★ Bob's your uncle. …………………………… 易如反掌。/ 一切顺利。
★ This job was handed to me on a silver plate.
…………………………………………… 我不需要努力就获得了这份工作。
★ This is an open-and-shut case. ………………… 这件事很简单。
  open-and-shut 表示"一目了然的、很简单的"
★ I can do this with one hand tied behind my back.
…………………………………………… 这件事对我来说轻而易举。
★ I sailed through the test. ……………………… 我顺利通过了考试。
  sail through 表示"顺利通过"
★ I think nothing of staying up all night. …………… 我觉得熬夜没什么。
  think nothing of 表示"视……为平常"
★ I can do this standing on my head. ………… 我可以轻易完成这件事。
★ He can fix his car with his eyes closed.
……………………………………… 他不费吹灰之力就可以修好他的车。
★ Is there a painless way to learn a language?
  painless 表示"容易的、轻松的" ……………… 学语言有轻松的方法吗?

### 听美国人聊天

**A** Is the math test hard? 数学考试难吗?
**B** No. It's a piece of cake. 不难。很简单。

---

**A** Thank you for helping me. 谢谢你帮助我。
**B** No problem. 别客气。

---

**A** Do you know how to make a cheesecake?
你知道要怎么做奶酪蛋糕吗?
**B** Yes. It's a cinch. 知道,这简单得很。

---

**A** I sailed through the test. 我顺利通过了考试。
**B** Well done. 做得好。

---

**A** How is your new job going? 你的新工作怎么样呢?
**B** It's a cushy job. 这工作很轻松。

---

**A** Is there a painless way to learn a language?
学语言有轻松的方法吗?
**B** No. It takes time and effort to master a foreign language.
没有。需要时间与努力才能精通一种外语。

---

**A** I'm on a diet now and trying to lose some weight.
我现在在节食,希望能够减些体重。
**B** Losing weight is not difficult. You need to get more exercise. 减重并不难,你需要增加运动。

---

**A** I don't know how to cook or clean.
我不会煮饭或是做清洁工作。
**B** Come on. It's not rocket science.
来吧,这又不是什么难事。

**相关会话群组记忆**　表达"事情或处境很困难、复杂、艰难"

★ **It's not easy.** 任何情况皆适用 ……………… 这不容易。
★ **It's difficult for me.** ……………… 这对我来说很困难。
★ **It's difficult to tell the truth.** ……… 说实话很困难。
★ **It's hard to save money.** ………………… 存钱很难。
★ **This is an arduous training.**
　　arduous 表示"艰巨的、艰苦的"……… 这是一项艰苦的训练。
★ **It's complicated.** ……………………………… 这很复杂。
★ **It's no cinch.** ……………………… 这不是容易的事。
★ **It's no picnic.** ……………………………… 这并不轻松。
　　picnic 表示"轻松的工作"
★ **It's a bit tricky.** ……………………… 这有一点棘手。
★ **It's very challenging.** ……………… 这非常有挑战性。
★ **It's taxing work.** ………………… 这是一个费力的工作。
★ **It's a laborious assignment.** 这是一个吃力的工作。
★ **This is a tough decision.** …… 这是一个艰难的决定。
★ **Mountain climbing is very strenuous.**
　　strenuous 表示"费力的"……………………… 登山非常费力。

★ **This is no joke.** ……………………… 这不是闹着玩。
★ **It's not a walk in the park.** ………… 这并不是一件容易的事。
★ **That's a toughie.** ……………………… 这是个难题。
★ **This project is a little problematic.** ·· 这个计划有一些麻烦。
　　problematic 表示"成问题的、疑难的"
★ **It's a demanding job.** ……………… 这是一份吃力的工作。
★ **Our teacher is very demanding.** ……… 我们的老师很严苛。

★ These are puzzling questions. 这些都是令人费解的问题。

    puzzling 表示"费解的"

★ We finally finished this exacting task. 我们终于完成了这项艰巨的任务。

★ This is an onerous burden for me.

    onerous 表示"繁重的" 这对我来说是个繁重的负担。

★ The noise is murder. 这噪声真要命。

★ They are formidable warriors. 他们是难以对付的战士。

★ Life is an uphill journey. 生命是一场艰难的旅程。

★ There are so many knotty problems to deal with.

    knotty 表示"难解决的" 有许多棘手的问题要处理。

★ This is a thorny situation. 这是一个棘手的局面。

---

★ Life is not always a bed of roses. 人生并非总是称心如意。
★ I had a hard / rough time. 我有过一段困难的时期。
★ The company was in deep water. 公司遭遇困难。
★ John has been in hot water recently. 约翰这阵子遇到困难。
★ I'm in a fix.   fix 表示"困境" 我处于困境。
★ I have a devil of a job of getting up early. 我早起有困难。
★ She was like a fish out of water in this place.

    她在这个地方感到不自在。

★ Mr. Wales is a hard nut to crack. 威尔斯先生是个难对付的人。
★ This question is a hard nut to crack. 这个问题很棘手。
★ It's easier said than done. 说时容易做时难。
★ I'm in a quandary.   quandary 表示"困境" 我左右为难。
★ I'm between a rock and a hard place now. 我现在进退两难。
★ It's a can of worms. 这是个复杂的问题。
★ You can't teach an old dog new tricks. 老狗学不了新把戏。
★ There are wheels within wheels. 局面错综复杂。
★ It's too much like hard work. 这太累人了。
★ We finished the job the hard way. 我们费一番功夫才完成工作。

**听美国人聊天**

A How is your project coming along? 你的计划进行得如何？
B This project is a little problematic. 这个计划有一些麻烦。

---

A Teaching is not an easy job. 教书不是一份容易的工作。
B Well, practice makes perfect. 嗯，熟能生巧。

---

A Do you like your new job? 你喜欢你的新工作吗？
B Not really. It's quite demanding. 不怎么喜欢，工作很严苛。

---

A Life is not always a bed of roses. 人生不总是称心如意。
B I agree. We just have to go with the flow.
我同意，我们只需顺其自然。

---

A If you eat less and exercise more, then you will lose weight.
如果你少吃多动，那么你就能减肥了。
B It's easier said than done. 说比做容易。

---

A I had a hard time recently. 我最近日子不好过。
B Cheer up! Everything will be all right.
振作一点！一切都会没事。

---

A There are so many knotty problems to deal with and I don't have enough time.
我有太多棘手的问题要处理，但时间却不够。
B You should manage your time effectively.
你应该有效率地运用你的时间。

---

A I don't know if I should quit my job. 我不知道我是否应该辞职。
B This is a tough decision. 这是个艰难的决定。

(美国人还会这样说) **其他与表达"非常容易"相关的惯用语**

### 1. like shooting fish in a barrel 很简单的事

barrel 意思是"桶子",字面上的意思是"如同在桶子里射鱼",比喻为"很简单的事"。

- For me, learning to play piano is like shooting fish in a barrel.

  对我来说,学钢琴是很简单的事。

### 2. like taking candy from a baby 轻而易举

字面上的意思是"如同从婴儿手中拿走糖果",比喻为"轻而易举"。

- For him, doing a one arm push-up is like taking candy from a baby.

  对他来说,单手做俯卧撑是轻而易举的事。

### 3. could do something in one's sleep 事情很简单

字面上的意思是"可在睡觉时做某件事",比喻为"事情很简单"。

- I've done it many times. I could do it in my sleep.

  我做这件事很多次了,这件事对我来说很简单。

# Lesson 25  A Smart Cookie

## 很聪明的人

Part 3 美国人聊天都说这些话

 中文"很聪明的人",英语要如何表达呢?

就是"a smart cookie"。smart 表示"聪明的",但是"a smart cookie"意思可不是"一块聪明的饼干",跟饼干没有关系。cookie 除了表示"饼干",在这句惯用语中则是"人"的意思。因此"a smart cookie"意思就是"一个聪明的人"。当你要形容某人很聪明时,即可使用"a smart cookie"。

- She is quite a smart cookie.
  她真是个聪明人。

- George is called a smart cookie.
  乔治被称为聪明人。

- I like her because she is a smart cookie.
  我喜欢她因为她很聪明。

- He has answers to all my questions. He is such a smart cookie.
  他能回答我所有问题。他真的很聪明。

- I'm surprised that a smart cookie like you can't figure it out.
  我很惊讶像你这么聪明的人竟然无法明白。

- That kid is a smart cookie. He learns things quickly.
  那个小孩非常聪明。他学习很快。

**相关会话群组记忆** 表达"聪明、才智"

★ **He is smart.** ⌒任何情况皆适用 ……… 他很聪明。
★ **He is a clever boy.** …………… 他是个聪明的男孩。
★ **He is a wise man.** ……………… 他是个有智慧的人。
★ **This is a wise decision.** ……… 这是个明智的决定。
★ **She is such a brilliant girl.**
 …………………………………… 她是一个如此聪明的女孩。
★ **She has a brilliant mind.** …… 她头脑很聪明。
★ **What a brilliant show!** ……… 真是精彩的表演!
 ⌒ brilliant 表示"聪明的、出色的"
★ **You are a genius!** ……………………… 你是天才!
★ **He is a gifted sculptor.** …… 他是一名有天赋的雕刻家。
★ **He has the wit to solve the problem.**
 ⌒ wit 表示"智慧" ………………… 他有解决问题的智慧。
★ **This kid is talented.** …………… 这个小孩很有天分。
★ **She is a woman of diverse talents.**
 ……………………………………… 她是个多才多艺的女子。
★ **She has an agile mind.** ……… 她思维敏捷。
★ **She has such a nimble and creative mind.**
 ⌒ nimble 表示"聪明的、机智的" ……… 她头脑聪明且有创意。
★ **He is a shrewd businessman.**
 ……………………………………… 他是一名精明的商人。
★ **I admire him for his intellect.** …… 我钦佩他的才智。
★ **She is an independent and intelligent woman.**
 ……………………………………… 她是一个独立且聪明的女子。
★ **My boyfriend has a high IQ.** … 我男朋友的智商很高。

★ **This boy has so much intelligence.**
这个男孩有许多聪明才智。

★ **My girlfriend is very intellectual.**
我女朋友很聪明。

★ **He is the most resourceful man I've ever met.**
他是我遇到过的最足智多谋的人。

★ **She is very savvy and sophisticated.**
她非常有见识且世故。

★ **These are words of wisdom.** 这些是智慧之语。

★ **He is a canny politician.** 他是一个精明的政客。

★ **Kurt is an astute lawyer and has never lost a case.** 科特是一位精明的律师,他从未输过一场官司。

★ **He is a crafty liar.** 他是个狡猾的说谎者。

★ **He is a sharp salesman.** 他是一个精明的推销员。

  sharp 表示"精明的、狡猾的"

★ **Dr. Liu is knowledgeable about English literature.** 刘博士精通英国文学。

★ **The manager is very sagacious.** 经理非常睿智。

★ **He is adept at playing guitar.** 他擅长弹吉他。

---

★ He is clear-sighted. 他很聪明。
  clear-sighted 表示"聪明的"

★ She is quick-witted. 她很机智。
  quick-witted 表示"机智的"

★ He is quick to learn things. 他学东西很快。
  quick 表示"敏捷的"

★ She is quick on the uptake. 她理解力强。
  uptake 表示"领会"

★ Natasha is quick on the trigger. ············ 娜塔莎反应敏捷。

  ↳ trigger 表示 "扳机"; quick on the trigger 表示 "反应敏捷的、机灵的"

★ He is a well-educated young man.

  ↳ well-educated 表示 "有教养的" ········ 他是一个有教养的年轻人。

★ I am well-versed in chemistry. ····················· 我精通化学。

  ↳ versed 表示 "精通的"; well-versed 表示 "精通的"

★ Stop being clever-clever. ················ 不要再卖弄小聪明了。

  ↳ clever-clever 表示 "卖弄小聪明的"

★ Jennifer is too clever by half. ············ 珍妮弗聪明过头了。

  ↳ too clever by half 表示 "聪明过头的、卖弄小聪明的"

★ Some bright spark forgot to turn off the light.

  ····································· 某个聪明的家伙忘了关灯。

----------------------------------------- 25-04

★ I wasn't born yesterday. ······························ 我不是傻瓜。

  ↳ 这句字面上的意思是 "我不是昨天才出生",形容一个人 "不是傻瓜、很世故" 的意思

★ My niece is as bright as a button. ··············· 我的侄女非常聪明伶俐。

  ↳ 这句字面上意思是 "如纽扣般闪亮",形容一个人 "聪明伶俐" 的意思

★ He had his head screwed on. ································ 他头脑清醒。

★ He always used his remarkable grey matter to solve many problems. ·························· 他总是运用他非凡的才智解决许多问题。

★ The new staff is really on the ball. ····················· 新员工非常机灵。

  ↳ on the ball 表示 "机灵的、高明的"

★ Eleanor is very well-informed. ···················· 艾莉诺非常见多识广。

★ Marianne is nobody's fool. ···························· 玛莉安娜为人精明。

  ↳ fool 表示 "傻子"; nobody's fool 表示 "为人精明"

★ Is he all there? ··················································· 他神志清醒吗?

★ He has a lot of horse sense. ························· 他知道很多常识。

  ↳ horse sense 表示 "普通常识"

★ Walter is really a walking encyclopedia.

  ································· 沃尔特简直是一部活的百科全书。

**听美国人聊天**

**A** What do you think of our new manager?
你觉得新来的经理怎么样?
**B** I think he is really on the ball. 我觉得他真的非常出色。

**A** Toby can speak seven languages. 托比会说七种语言。
**B** He is quick to learn things. 他学东西很快。

**A** Janice is so smart. She can answer any question.
珍妮丝很聪明,可以回答任何问题。
**B** She is really a walking encyclopedia.
她简直是一部活的百科全书。

**A** Ben is adept at playing the piano and guitar.
本擅长弹钢琴与吉他。
**B** He is so talented. 他真有才华。

**A** Do you know how to open a can? 你知道怎么开罐头吗?
**B** Of course! I wasn't born yesterday. 当然!我又不是傻瓜。

**A** Why don't we ask Professor Hopkins about this? He is an expert in history. 我们何不问霍普金斯教授,他是历史专家。
**B** This is a good idea. 这是个好办法。

**A** I decided to apologize to my mother. 我决定向我母亲道歉。
**B** This is a wise decision. 这是个明智的决定。

**A** This is a persuasive speech. 这是一场有说服力的演讲。
**B** It is, and the speaker is quick-witted.
的确,而且演讲者非常机智。

Part 3 美国人聊天都说这些话

(相关会话群组记忆) 表达"不聪明、愚笨的、愚蠢的"

MP3 25-05

★ **Don't be stupid.** 别傻了。
★ **It's so stupid.** 这真愚蠢。
★ **I made a stupid mistake.** 我犯了一个愚蠢的错误。
★ **It's a silly thing to do.** 这么做很傻。
★ **This idea sounds dumb.** 这个想法听起来很蠢。
★ **She is too dumb to work it out.** 她太笨以至于找不到解决方法。
  ↳ dumb 表示"愚蠢的"
★ **You are a dummy.** 你是个笨蛋。
  ↳ dummy 表示"笨蛋"
★ **She is such a fool.** 她真是个傻子。
★ **You are so foolish.** 你真是傻。
★ **He is a silly boy.** 他是个傻男孩。
★ **He is a bit thick / dense.** 他有点儿蠢 / 愚笨。
★ **She is a dimwit.** 她是个傻子。
★ **He is a real schmuck.** 他真是个笨蛋。
  ↳ schmuck 表示"笨蛋"
★ **He is a chump.** 他是个傻瓜。
★ **He is a goofy person.** 他是个傻瓜。
★ **This is very unwise.** 这非常不明智。
★ **He is an obtuse man.** 他是一个愚钝的人。
★ **This is so absurd.** 这太愚蠢可笑了。
★ **It's extremely ridiculous.** 这真是非常可笑。
  ↳ ridiculous 表示"荒谬的、可笑的"
★ **Your question is preposterous.** 你的问题十分荒谬。

★ She is not all there. ..................................... 她神志不清。
★ Don't talk drivel. ↝ drivel 表示"傻话、蠢话" ......... 别说傻话。
★ He is a complete airhead. ..................... 他是一个大笨蛋。
★ She is an empty-headed girl. ............. 她是个愚笨的女孩。
★ Nancy is a simple-minded and naive girl.
..................................................... 南希是个头脑简单且天真的女孩。
★ He is slow on the uptake. ................................ 他理解慢。
★ He is a bit slow-witted. ........................... 他有一点儿迟钝。
  ↝ slow-witted 表示"笨的、迟钝的"
★ This decision is ill-advised. ................. 这个决定欠缺考虑。
★ He is thick as two short planks. ................... 他非常愚笨。
★ She is (as) daft as a brush. ........................ 她非常愚蠢。
★ The lights are on but no his home. .......... 他不是很聪明。
★ His elevator doesn't go to the top floor. ......... 他不聪明。

★ He is not the brightest bulb / crayon in the box. ............. 他不聪明。
★ He is not the brightest star in the sky. ........................ 他不聪明。
★ He is not the sharpest tool in the shed. ...................... 他不聪明。
  ↝ sharpest 表示"最锐利的";shed 表示"(放工具的)棚屋"
★ He is not the sharpest knife in the drawer. ................... 他不聪明。
★ He is a few cards short of a full deck. ......................... 他不聪明。
★ He is a few colors short of a rainbow. ......................... 他不聪明。
★ He is a few clowns short of a circus. .......................... 他不聪明。
  ↝ 字面意思是"缺了几个小丑的马戏团"
★ He is a few fries short of a Happy Meal. ...................... 他不聪明。
★ He is a few sandwiches short of a picnic. .................... 他不聪明。
★ He has nothing between his ears. .............................. 他不聪明。
  ↝ 也可以说成 He doesn't have much between his ears.
★ He is dead from the neck up. ..................................... 他很愚蠢。

## 美国人还会这样说

**A** Why do you look so worried today?
你今天看起来怎么这么烦恼?

**B** I left my cell phone in a taxi. This is so stupid!
我把手机落在出租车上了。这真是愚蠢!

---

**A** I can't believe he decided to quit. 我真不敢相信他决定要辞职。

**B** This is very unwise. 这非常不明智。

---

**A** Roy is such a big liar. 罗伊真会说谎。

**B** I'm a fool to trust him. 我真是傻才会相信他。

---

**A** Why does he always screw things up?
他为什么总是把事情搞砸? → screw up 表示"搞砸某事"

**B** His lights are on but no one's home.
他不是很聪明。

---

**A** Why do you call him a schmuck? 你为什么说他是笨蛋?

**B** Because he is a few cards short of a full deck.
因为他不聪明。

---

**A** I picked up the wrong kid from school today.
我今天在学校接错了小孩。

**B** It's so ridiculous. 真夸张。

---

**A** He is not the brightest bulb in the box. 他并不聪明。

**B** That's why he always makes the same mistake.
这就是为什么他老是犯同样的错误。

---

**A** My son thinks Santa Claus is real. 我儿子认为圣诞老人是真的。

**B** He is so naive. 他真是天真。

**美国人还会这样说** 其他与表达"一个人很聪明"相关的惯用语

## 1. smart as a whip 很聪明

whip 是"鞭子"的意思,这句字面意思是"如鞭子一样聪明"。形容一个人非常聪明、聪慧灵巧的意思。

- She is smart as a whip and learns fast.
  她非常聪明,学东西快。

## 2. sharp as a razor 非常机灵

sharp 是"锐利"的意思,razor 是"剃刀"的意思。这句字面意思是"像剃刀一样锐利",用来比喻一个人非常机灵。

- He is sharp as a razor. We can always count on him.
  他非常机灵,我们总是可以依靠他。

## 3. have a good head on one's shoulders 聪明有见识

这句字面意思是"肩膀上有一颗好头颅",用来比喻一个人有头脑、很聪明、有见识。

- He has a good head on his shoulders and he can solve any problem.
  他聪明有见识,能够解决任何问题。

# Lesson 26 Break a Leg

## 祝你好运

中文"祝你好运",英语要如何表达呢?

就是"break a leg"。break 表示"折断",leg 表示"腿",字面上的意思是"断一条腿"。这句话源自一种迷信,并不是真的希望别人断一条腿,而是祝福别人演出成功或是祝好运的意思。因此,要祝福别人成功或好运时,可用"break a leg"这个短语。

- I hope you break a leg.
  祝你好运。

- Break a leg. Everything will be fine.
  祝你好运,一切都会没事的。

- Break a leg. I hope the performance goes well.
  祝你好运,希望表演顺利。

- Break a leg. I'm sure you will do an excellent job.
  祝你好运,我确定你会做得很好。

- I'm sorry you've been sick. I hope you will get better soon. Break a leg.
  很难过你最近生病了,希望你赶快好转,祝你好运。

- My friends told me to break a leg before I went onto the stage.
  我朋友在我走上舞台之前祝我好运。

（相关会话群组记忆） 表达"祝好运、幸运、把握良机"

★ **Good luck. / Good luck to you.** ⌒ 任何情况皆适用
  ........................................................... 祝好运。/ 祝你好运。
★ **Good luck with your new job.** ....... 祝新工作顺利。
★ **God bless you.** .................................... 愿上帝保佑你。
★ **I wish you luck.** .................................... 祝你好运。
★ **Wishing you lots of luck.** ............. 祝你有很多好运。
★ **I am blessed.** ........................................ 我很幸运。
★ **Lucky you. / Lucky me.** ........ 你真幸运。/ 我真幸运。
★ **How lucky you are.** ............................. 你真幸运。
★ **You're in luck.** ...................................... 你运气真好。
★ **You lucky thing.** ............................. 你这个幸运的家伙。
★ **You'll do great!** ..................................... 你会很棒！
★ **It was pure luck.** ............................... 这纯粹是侥幸。
★ **It was just a fluke.** ⌒ 较口语 ............... 这纯属侥幸。
★ **It's a piece of luck.** ....................... 这是一件幸运的事。
★ **You are so fortunate.** ........................... 你真幸运。
  ⌒ fortunate 表示"幸运的"
★ **You're so lucky. / You are very lucky.**
  ........................................................................... 你真幸运。
★ **I'm well-off.** ............................................ 我很幸运。

★ Any luck? .................................... 运气怎么样？/ 事成了吗？
★ Did you have any luck today? ............... 你今天运气如何？
★ The charm is for luck. ........................ 护身符是为了吉利。

★ Don't push your luck. ……别再碰运气了。
  - push one's luck 表示"为了再度走运而冒险"
★ I just lucked out. ……我只是运气好。
  - luck out 表示"走运、侥幸成功"
★ We struck it lucky this time. ……我们这次运气好。
  - strike it lucky 表示"运气好"
★ This was a stroke of luck. ……这真是意外的好运。
★ This must be your lucky day. ……今天一定是你的幸运日。
★ You're a lucky dog. ……你是个幸运的家伙。
  - lucky dog 表示"幸运儿"
★ It's a lucky break. ……没想到运气这么好。
  - lucky break 表示"没料到的幸运事"
★ Luck is on your side. ……好运在你身边。
★ Hope everything goes well with you. ……祝你一切顺利。
★ May you have good fortune. ……祝你好运。
★ I'm having a charmed life. ……我的人生很幸运。
  - charmed 表示"如有神保佑的"
★ She has a fortunate life. ……她有幸运的人生。

---

★ Knock on wood. ……祈求好运。
★ Touch wood. ……祈求好运。
★ Everything is coming up roses. ……一切都很顺利。
★ Knock them dead. ……祝好运。
★ Keep your fingers crossed. ……祈求好运。
★ I'll keep my fingers crossed for you. ……我祝福你。
★ Keep your fingers crossed for me. ……请祝我好运。
★ That's the luck of the draw. ……这要靠运气。
★ You can try your luck at it. ……你可以碰运气看看。
  - try your luck at sth. 表示"碰运气"
★ Some people have all the luck. ……有些人运气就是很好。

- ★ It's third time lucky. …… 第三次就会走运了。
- ★ I have a lucky streak. …… 我运气很好。
- ★ I'm on a lucky streak. …… 我运气很好。
  - streak 表示"一连串";lucky streak 表示"运气好"
- ★ It's just beginner's luck. …… 这纯粹是新手的好运气。
- ★ You can thank your lucky stars. …… 你真幸运。
- ★ Fortune smiles on you. …… 你运气很好。
- ★ Fortune smiles on our team. …… 我们团队运气很好。
- ★ It's a blessing in disguise. …… 因祸得福。
- ★ I'm sitting pretty. …… 我处境幸运。
  - sitting pretty 表示"处境幸运"
- ★ I'm on a roll. …… 我现在好运连连。
  - on a roll 表示"好运连连"
- ★ It's a good job that everything is fine. …… 幸好一切都没事。
  - good job 表示"幸运的事"
- ★ It's a good thing that no one was hurt. …… 很幸运没有人受伤。
- ★ I'm in the groove. …… 我处于最佳状态。
- ★ He held all the aces. …… 他占有绝对优势。
- ★ Luckily / Fortunately, my wallet was found. …… 幸运的是,我的皮夹找到了。
- ★ The show hit it big. …… 表演非常成功。
  - hit it big 表示"非常成功"
- ★ It's lucky / fortunate that the weather is fine. …… 幸运的是天气很好。
- ★ With any luck, we will finish the job tomorrow. …… 幸运的话,我们将在明天完成工作。
- ★ It was just as well that you told me the truth. …… 幸好你告诉了我实话。
  - just as well 表示"幸好"
- ★ He was born with a silver spoon in his mouth. …… 他出身富贵。
- ★ I can always land / fall on my feet no matter what. …… 无论如何,我总是能够逢凶化吉。
- ★ The outcome is in the lap of gods. …… 结果难以预料。
- ★ This is a mixed blessing. …… 这是一件好坏参半的事情。
- ★ Better luck next time. …… 下次运气一定会更好。
  - 这句是用来鼓励在某些事失败的人

Part 3 美国人聊天都说这些话

### 听美国人聊天

A  I'm taking the TOEIC test tomorrow. 我明天要参加托业考试。
B  Good luck! 祝你好运!

---

A  My boyfriend gave me the silent treatment for a week.
   我男朋友跟我冷战一个星期了。
   → silent treatment 是"沉默的对待""冷战"的意思

B  Well, good luck with that. 嗯,祝你好运。

---

A  Fiona will have surgery to remove a breast tumor today.
   菲奥娜今天要动外科手术移除胸部肿瘤。
   → surgery 是"外科手术"的意思;tumor 是"肿瘤"的意思

B  Keep your fingers crossed for her. 祈求她有好运。

---

A  I have never been sick in my life. 我这辈子从来没生过病。
B  Knock on wood. 老天保佑。

---

A  I failed the driving test two times. 我驾照考了两次都没过。
B  Well, the third time's the charm. 嗯,第三次会有好运气的。

---

A  The girl was born with a silver spoon in her mouth.
   这个女孩出身富贵。
B  Some people have all the luck. 有些人运气就是很好。

---

A  Fortunately, my wallet was found. 幸运的是,我的皮夹找到了。
B  This must be your lucky day. 这一定是你的幸运日。

---

A  I can't believe I won the lottery twice in a row!
   我真不敢相信我连中彩票两次! → in a row 表示"连续地"

B  You're really on a roll. 你真是好运连连。

**相关会话群组记忆** 表达"运气不好、倒霉、错失良机"

26-05

★ **Bad luck! / It's bad luck!** ……… 运气不好!
★ **Tough luck.** ……… 真不幸。/ 真倒霉。/ 运气不好。
　↳ tough 表示"不幸的"
★ **Hard luck.** ……… 运气真不好。
★ **It's hard luck on him.** ……… 他运气真不好。
★ **Worse luck!** ……… 真可惜!
★ **Just my luck!** ……… 我真倒霉!
★ **No such luck.** ……… 没这个运气。
★ **I'm unlucky.** ……… 我很倒霉。
★ **It is unlucky to break a mirror.**
　……… 打破镜子很不吉利。
★ **This is a serious mischance.**
　↳ mischance 表示"不幸、厄运" ……… 这是一个重大的不幸事件。
★ **He might be the most luckless man I've ever met.** ……… 他可能是我遇见过的最倒霉的人。
★ **Today is a luckless day.** ……… 今天真是不幸的一天。
★ **I'm totally hopeless.** ……… 我彻底没希望了。

26-06

★ What rotten luck! ……… 真倒霉!
★ I was out of luck. ……… 我运气不好。
　↳ out of luck 表示"运气不好、不走运"
★ My luck was out. ……… 我运气不好。
★ I'm down on my luck lately. ……… 我最近很倒霉。
　↳ down on one's luck 表示"某人很倒霉"
★ Today is not my day. ……… 今天真倒霉。

- ★ Hard cheese! —— 真倒霉！
- ★ Fat chance! —— 没机会！/ 不可能！
- ★ He is a jinx. —— 他是个倒霉鬼。
- ★ It's a jinx. ☞ jinx 表示"不祥之人/物" —— 这不吉利。
- ★ He has been jinxed recently. —— 他最近很倒霉。
- ★ He has been suffering from misfortune.

  ☞ misfortune 表示"厄运" —— 他最近遭遇了厄运
- ★ You can donate money to help unfortunate people.

  —— 你可以捐钱帮助不幸的人们。
- ★ This is an unfortunate accident. —— 这是一个不幸的事件。
- ★ Unfortunately, I was wrong. —— 不幸的是，我错了。
- ★ Something untoward happened to him.

  —— 他发生了一些不幸的事情。

26-07

- ★ No luck. —— 运气不好。
- ★ I had no luck today. —— 我今天运气不好。
- ★ As luck would have it, the concert was rained out.

  —— 不幸的是，演唱会因雨延期。
- ★ I had a run of bad luck recently. —— 我最近厄运连连。

  ☞ a run of bad luck 表示"一连串倒霉的事"
- ★ That ship has sailed. —— 为时已晚。
- ★ I drew the short straw. —— 我抽到下下签。
- ★ We should help those hapless people.

  ☞ hapless 表示"不幸的" —— 我们应该帮助那些不幸的人。
- ★ She encountered a series of miserable events recently.

  —— 她最近遭遇到一连串悲惨的事。
- ★ He is behind the eight ball now. —— 他目前遇到挫折。
- ★ I won't leave you in the lurch. —— 我不会将你弃于困境。
- ★ We missed the boat this time. —— 我们这次错过了良机。
- ★ He had an ill-starred / ill-fated life. —— 他生活得很悲惨。

  ☞ ill-starred 表示"不幸的、运气不佳的"

## 听美国人聊天

**A** You look awful. What's wrong? 你看起来糟透了，怎么了？
→ awful 表示"很糟的"；rob 表示"抢劫"

**B** I was robbed. It was just my luck! 我被抢劫了，真倒霉！

---

**A** Today is not my day. I feel sick and I can't do anything.
今天真倒霉，我身体不舒服，什么事都做不了。

**B** You should just stay home. 你应该待在家就好。

---

**A** Every time I don't bring an umbrella, it rains. That must be Murphy's Law. 每次我没带伞，一定会下雨。这一定是墨菲定律。

**B** You've got a point there. 你说得有道理。

---

**A** My baggage was lost at the airport. 我的行李在机场不见了。

**B** Bad luck. 运气真差。

---

**A** Yesterday I got a ticket again! 我昨天又被开罚单了！

**B** Hard luck! 真倒霉！

---

**A** The teacher flunked me. 老师让我不及格。
→ flunk 表示"使不及格"

**B** You're really out of luck. 你运气真不好。

---

**A** I sprained my ankle while playing basketball.
我打篮球的时候扭伤脚踝。

**B** Tough luck for you. 你真倒霉。

---

**A** I had a run of bad luck recently. 我最近厄运不断。

**B** Don't worry. I'm sure everything will be fine.
别烦恼，我确定一切都会没事。

**美国人还会这样说** 其他与表达"好运"相关的惯用语

## 1. strike while the iron is hot 把握良机

strike 意思是"打、敲",这句字面意思是"趁热打铁",形容做事情要"把握良机"。

- You should strike while the iron is hot or you will miss the boat.
  你应该趁热打铁,否则你会错失良机。

## 2. make hay while the sun shines 勿错失机会

hay 意思是"干草",make hay 意思是"晒干草",这句字面意思是"趁有阳光时晒干草",比喻"勿错失机会"。

- Make hay while the sun shines because time waits for no man.
  勿错失机会,因为时间不等人。

## 3. while the going is good 把握机会

going 意思是"进展、情况",这句字面意思是"趁形势大好时",比喻"要把握机会"。

- The protesters retreated while the going is good.
  抗议者趁形势大好时撤退。

# Lesson 27　Up in the Air

## 事情悬而未决

中文"事情悬而未决",英语要如何表达呢?

就是"up in the air"。air 是"天空、空中"的意思。这句短语字面上的意思是"悬在空中"。比喻事情还没解决、尚未决定。因此,若要描述一件事情悬而未决,即可使用"up in the air"这个短语,也可以说成"in the air"。

- Our plan is up in the air.
  我们的计划悬而未决。

- This case is still up in the air.
  这件事情仍悬而未决。

- Whether I go or not is up in the air.
  我尚未决定是否要去。

- The final result remains up in the air.
  最后结果尚未确定。

- Everything is up in the air and I have to make a decision.
  一切都悬而未决,我必须做个决定。

- When the meeting begins is up in the air.
  会议尚不知何时开始。

- The course schedule is up in the air.
  课程进度表尚未确定。

(相关会话群组记忆) 表达"悬而未决、不确定的、有疑问的"

27-02

★ **I don't know.** ……………………………… 我不知道。
★ **I don't know whether he will accept my invitation.** ………… 我不知道他是否会接受我的邀请。
★ **I'm not sure.** ☜任何情况皆适用 ……………… 我不确定。
★ **I'm not sure about / of it.** …………… 我对此不确定。
★ **I'm not sure whether I like him or not.**
……………………………………… 我不确定是否喜欢他。
★ **I'm uncertain about this.** ………… 我对此不确定。
★ **I'm uncertain whether he will come or not.**
……………………………………… 我不确定他是否会来。
★ **The result is uncertain.** ……………… 结果难以预料。
★ **I'm unclear about it.** ………………… 我对此不清楚。
★ **I'm unclear why he did this.**
……………………………………… 我不明白他为什么这么做。
★ **I'm unclear whether he is angry or not.**
……………………………………… 我不清楚他是否在生气。
★ **I doubt it.** …………………………… 我不信。/ 我不这么认为。
★ **I doubt whether he is right or not.**
……………………………………… 我怀疑他是否是对的。
★ **I have doubts about it.** ……………… 我对此有疑虑。
★ **The whole thing is in doubt.** …… 整件事都有疑虑。
★ **If in doubt, don't.**
……………………………………… 如果有疑虑,就不要做。
★ **I'm dubious about getting married.**
……………………………………… 我对结婚犹豫不决。

- ★ You never know. *较口语* —— 很难说。/ 很难预料。
- ★ I guess so. —— 我想是吧。
- ★ I suppose so. *suppose 表示"猜想、推测"* —— 我想是吧。
- ★ I don't think so. —— 我不这么认为。
- ★ It's unlikely to be true. —— 这不太可能是真的。
- ★ Perhaps he won't come today. —— 他今天可能不会来。
- ★ Maybe she's wrong. —— 也许她是错的。
- ★ He probably missed the train. —— 他大概是错过火车了。
- ★ It might be true. —— 这可能是真的。
- ★ I could possibly be pregnant. —— 我有可能是怀孕了。
- ★ I'm doubtful about what he said. —— 我对他说的感到怀疑。
- ★ Life is changeable. —— 生命充满变化。
- ★ I can't make up my mind. —— 我没办法做决定。
- ★ I haven't decided yet. —— 我尚未决定。
- ★ I can't decide whether it's a good idea or not.
  —— 我没办法决定这是否是好主意。
- ★ This theory is questionable. —— 这个理论未必正确。
- ★ It's questionable whether this theory can be put into practice. —— 无法确定这项理论是否能够付诸实践。
- ★ It is unknown to me. —— 我对此不了解。
- ★ I'm still undecided as to which dress I should wear.
  —— 我还没决定穿哪件连衣裙。
- ★ The cause of her death is undetermined.
  —— 她的死因不明。
- ★ There are many troublesome unsettled arguments.
  —— 有许多麻烦的事未解决争议。
- ★ He made a chancy decision. —— 他做了一个没有把握的决定。
  *chancy 表示"没把握的、不确定的"*

★ It is a disputable question. ……… 这是一个有争议的问题。

   disputable 表示"有争议的"

★ The rumor is unconfirmed. …………………… 谣言未经证实。
★ He gave me a vague explanation.

   ………………………………… 他给了我一个含糊的解释。

★ This book is so obscure. ……………………… 这本书很难理解。

   obscure 表示"费解的、复杂的"

★ Her musical career is iffy. ………… 她的音乐生涯很不确定。

(27-04)

★ The issue stills hangs in doubt. ……………… 这个争议仍悬而未决。
★ The problem is hanging in the scales. ……………… 此问题悬而未决。
★ The outcome is hanging in the balance. ……………… 结果悬而未决。
★ This is a pending issue. ……………… 这是一件悬而未决的事情。

   pending 表示"未定的、未决的"

★ It remains to be seen. …………………………………… 事情尚待分晓。
★ It's early days yet. ………………… 现在还言之过早。/ 还无法下定论。
★ The article is open to question. ……………… 这篇文章有讨论空间。
★ There's no knowing what will happen. …… 难以预料将会发生什么事。
★ I'm in two minds about it. …………………………… 我对此犹豫不决。

   in two minds 表示"犹豫不决"

★ I'll sleep on it. ……………………………………… 我好好考虑一下。
★ I'm in a quandary. ………………………………… 我感到犹豫不决。
★ Don't keep me in suspense. ……………………… 别让我悬着不安。
★ He has half a mind to quit his job. ……………………… 他有点儿想辞职。
★ He always shilly-shallies. ……………………………… 他总是踌躇不决。

   shilly-shally 表示"优柔寡断、犹豫不决"

★ I blow hot and cold about it. …………………………… 我对此摇摆不定。
★ Don't hem and haw. ………………… 别支支吾吾。/ 别犹豫不决。
★ The jury is still out on whether smoking causes lung cancer.

   ………………………………… 抽烟是否造成肺癌尚无定论。

**听美国人聊天**

**A** I can't believe she is not what she appears to be.
真不敢相信她表里不一。

**B** Well, you never know. 嗯，世事难料。

---

**A** Are you going to take this new job? 你要接受这个新工作吗？

**B** Let me sleep on it. 我考虑考虑。

---

**A** Is your wedding date set? 你婚礼日期定好了吗？

**B** I haven't decided yet. 我尚未决定。

---

**A** Do you really want a divorce? 你真的想离婚吗？

**B** I can't make up my mind. 我没办法做决定。

---

**A** I don't know if I should accept his proposal.
我不知道是否该接受他的求婚。 → proposal 表示"求婚"

**B** Don't hem and haw. Just say yes.
别犹豫了，就答应吧。

---

**A** Do you think that she had a nose job?
你觉得她有没有做鼻子整形？ → nose job 表示"鼻子整形手术"

**B** Yes. I suppose so. 我猜她做了。

---

**A** I'm still undecided as to which dress I should wear.
我还没决定该穿哪件连衣裙。

**B** The yellow one is great. 黄色那件很棒。

---

**A** I've been feeling sick in the morning recently.
我最近早上都觉得不舒服。

**B** You could possibly be pregnant. 你有可能是怀孕了。

Part 3 美国人聊天都说这些话

(相关会话群组记忆) 表达"事情确定的、清楚的、无疑问的"

★ **I'm sure.** 任何情况皆适用 ……………… 我确定。
★ **I'm sure about / of it.** ……………… 我对此很确定。
★ **I'm sure you are right.** ……………… 我确定你是对的。
★ **I'm quite / absolutely sure it was you.**
  ……………………………………… 我相当确定是你。
★ **I'm certain about / of it.** ……………… 我对此感到肯定。
★ **I'm certain that he is wrong.** ……… 我确定他错了。
★ **I'm clear about that.** ……………… 我很清楚这件事。
★ **It's clear that no one likes her.** … 显然没人喜欢她。
★ **Indeed.** ……………………………………… 确实。
★ **That's true.** ……………………………… 这是真的。
★ **I really did it.** ……………………… 我真的这么做了。
★ **All right.** ……………………………… 好。/ 可以。
★ **Of course I will go.** ……………… 我当然会去。

★ **By all means.** ……………………… 当然可以。/ 一定。
★ **I bet that he won't come.** ………… 我敢肯定他一定不会来。
★ **You bet!** ……………………………… 当然!/ 一定!
★ **I will for certain tell you the truth.** … 我一定会告诉你事实。
  ↳ for certain 表示"无疑地、肯定地"
★ **I'm confident of winning the game.** 我确信我能赢得比赛。
★ **I have no doubt about it.** ………… 我对此没有疑虑。
★ **Without (a) doubt, I can trust him.** … 无疑地,我能信任他。
★ **Beyond (a) doubt, I am wrong.** ………… 无疑地,我错了。
★ **We leave no doubt about it.** ……… 我们对此没有疑问。

★ His failure is inevitable. 他的失败是无可避免的。
★ The truth is incontestable. 真相是毋庸置疑的。
★ It's undeniable that he is pretty handsome.
  ↳ undeniable 表示"不可否认的" 不可否认的是他很帅。
★ I was doubtless wrong. 我无疑是错了。
★ I made a firm decision. 我做了一个果断的决定。
★ I'm assured of the result. 我对结果有信心。
★ The evidence of the crime is conclusive.
  ↳ conclusive 表示"确定的、确凿的" 犯罪的证据确凿。
★ She's a cinch to win the election. 她一定会被选上。
★ It's hard to change some deep-rooted habits.
  一些根深蒂固的习惯难以改变。
★ It's a clear-cut fact. 这是一个清楚的事实。
  ↳ clear-cut 表示"明确的、清楚的"

(27-07)

★ Obviously, you are a smart girl. 显然你是个聪明的女孩。
★ Definitely he will come. 他一定会来。
★ I will certainly do my best. 我一定会尽全力。
★ I'm positive about it. 我对此很确定。
★ I'm positive that you won't be disappointed. 我很肯定你不会失望。
★ It's as clear as day. 事情非常清楚。
  ↳ as clear as day 表示"显而易见的、一清二楚的"
★ It's as sure as eggs is eggs. 千真万确。/ 毫无疑问。
★ There is no two ways about it. 别无他法。/ 没有选择。
★ It's a black-and-white question. 这个问题黑白分明。
★ The die is cast. 木已成舟（骰子已经扔出去）。
★ I won't do it and that's flat. 我绝对不会这么做。
★ It's in the bag. 这是十拿九稳的事。
  ↳ in the bag 表示"十拿九稳的、稳操胜算的"
★ It's all cut-and-dried. 这都已成定局。
★ It's true beyond a shadow of a doubt. 这是千真万确的。

Part 3 美国人聊天都说这些话

## 听美国人聊天

**A** Would you come to my bachelor party?
你要来我的告别单身派对吗? → bachelor 表示"单身汉"
**B** You bet! 一定!

---

**A** Your point is very convincing. 你的观点很有说服力。
**B** Thank you. I just speak my mind.
谢谢你,我只是说出我心里的想法。

---

**A** Money is useful and necessary. 金钱很有用,也很必要。
**B** I agree. It's a clear-cut fact. 我同意,这是一个清楚的事实。

---

**A** Nobody likes to be cheated. 没有人喜欢被骗。
**B** That's true. 这是真的。

---

**A** Are you sure that the company will downsize?
你确定公司要裁员吗? → downsize 表示"裁员"
**B** I'm sure about it. 我很确定。

---

**A** Are you certain you want to move out?
你确定你想搬出去吗?
**B** Yes. I want to move out, and that's flat.
是的,我要搬出去,就这样。

---

**A** Apparently, he didn't do his best in this game.
他在这场比赛中显然没有做到最好。
**B** That's why he lost. 怪不得他比赛会输。

---

**A** I'm sure he will do a great job. 我确定他会做得很好。
**B** I have no doubt about it. 我不怀疑。

**美国人还会这样说** 其他与表达"悬而未决"相关的惯用语

## 1. sit on the fence 保持中立

fence 表示"篱笆",这个短语字面上的意思是"坐在篱笆上",表示"还在观望、考虑""还没做决定""保持中立"。

- She sat on the fence in this debate.
  她在这场辩论中保持中立。

## 2. not carved in stone 并非不能改变

carve 表示"雕刻",carved in stone 表示"刻在石头上",形容事情"永远不能改变"。not carved in stone 则表示"并非不能改变"。

- The new policies are not carved in stone yet.
  新政策并非不能改变。

## 3. chop and change 不断改变

chop 意思是"砍、劈",这个短语字面意思是"砍掉与改变",形容"不断改变心意"。

- If you always chop and change, you will miss many opportunities.
  如果你总是不断改变心意,你就会错过很多机会。

# Lesson 28  With Flying Colors

## 非常出色

🔴 中文"非常出色",英语要如何表达呢?

就是"with flying colors"。flying 表示"飘扬的",color 除了表示"颜色",还有"旗帜"的意思。这个短语字面上的意思是"飘扬的旗帜",代表胜利时飘扬着的旗帜,因此可引申为"表现得非常出色""非常成功""大获全胜"的意思。

- I passed the exam with flying colors.
  我考试成绩非常出色。

- She passed the audition with flying colors.
  她成功通过试镜。

- He finished the task with flying colors.
  他成功完成任务。

- We reached the sales goal with flying colors.
  我们成功达到销售目标。

- Alvin solved the problem with flying colors.
  阿尔文成功地解决了问题。

- The village survived the storm with flying colors.
  村庄安然度过了暴风雨。

- We have made it through the drought with flying colors.
  我们已安然度过了旱灾。

**相关会话群组记忆** 表达"表现出色、非常成功、大获全胜"

★ **Awesome! / Amazing! / Beautiful! / Good! / Excellent! / Great! / Marvelous! / Perfect! / Superb! / Terrific! / Wonderful!**
　　　　　　　　　　　　　很好！/ 棒极了！/ 了不起！

★ **Well done!** ← 任何情况皆适用 ……… 做得好！
★ **Good job!** ……………………………… 做得好！
★ **Good work!** …………………………… 做得好！
★ **Nice work!** …………………………… 做得好！
★ **Fantastic work!** ……………………… 真了不起！
★ **Nice going!** …………………………… 做得不错！
★ **Bravo!** ………………………………… 好极了！
★ **You did well.** ………………………… 你表现不错。
★ **Our company is doing well.** 我们公司经营得不错。
★ **Keep up the good work!** …………… 继续努力！
★ **Very impressive!** ………… 令人印象深刻！/ 很厉害！
★ **I'm impressed.** ………………………… 我很佩服。
★ **This is a phenomenal performance.**
　　↳ phenomenal 表示"杰出的、非凡的" …… 这是一个杰出的表演。
★ **The view is very breathtaking.** …… 景色非常壮观。
★ **Thumbs up!** …………………………………… 赞！
★ **Way to go!** …………………………… 做得好！
★ **You rock! / You rule!** ← 较口语 ……… 你太棒了！
★ **You're a professional.** ……………… 你是专家。
★ **You're the best.** ……………………… 你是最好的。
★ **You're sensational.** …………………… 你真是棒极了。

★ No one does it better than you. ……… 没人做得比你好。
★ You're really something. ……………… 你真了不起。
★ She has got it made. ………………… 她有成功的把握。
  ↳ have got it made 表示"有成功的把握"
★ You make a difference. ……………… 你很有影响力。
★ I'm so proud of you. ………………… 我为你感到骄傲。
★ The movie is a blockbuster. ………… 这部电影很卖座。
  ↳ blockbuster 表示"流行大片、轰动一时的事物"
★ I finally made it. ……………………… 我终于成功了。
★ You're a champ. ……………………… 你太棒了。
  ↳ champ 表示"冠军"
★ He aced his math test. ……………… 他数学考试得了高分。
★ I know you can do it. ………………… 我知道你做得到。
★ You're a winner. ……………………… 你是赢家。
★ He held all the aces in this game. … 他在比赛中占尽优势。

★ Everything was done smoothly. …………… 所有事情都顺利完成。
  ↳ smoothly 表示"顺利地"
★ It is an effortless job. ……………… 这是件不费力的工作。
★ The movie is a smash hit. ………………… 电影很成功。
  ↳ smash hit 表示"成功的演出、巨大的成功"
★ I did it with no trouble. ……………… 我轻而易举完成这件事。
★ It went like a dream. ………………… 事情十分顺利。
★ I finished the job without a hitch. … 我顺利完成此事。
  ↳ hitch 表示"障碍";without a hitch 表示"轻易地、非常顺利"
★ The wedding went like clockwork. ……… 婚礼进行得很顺利。
★ Now I'm getting somewhere. ……………… 现在我总算有所进展了。
  ↳ get somewhere 表示"有进展"
★ You're on the right track. ……………………… 你做对了。

**听美国人聊天**

A I've just completed a jigsaw puzzle. 我刚完成一幅拼图。
B Well done! 做得好！

---

A How did the plan go? 计划进行得如何？
B The plan came a long way. 计划已大有进展。

---

A I came second in the speech competition.
我演讲比赛得了第二名。 → come second 表示"得第二名"
B Good job! 做得好！

---

A J.K. Rowling is a very successful writer.
J·K·罗琳是一位非常成功的作家。
B I collected many of her books. 我收集了她好多书。

---

A How was the show last night? 昨天晚上的表演如何？
B The show brought the house down. 表演赢得满堂彩。

---

A I'm happy I aced my math test. 我很高兴我数学考试得高分。
B You did well. Keep up the good work.
你表现得很好，继续努力。

---

A She is a hard act to follow. 她的成功令人望尘莫及。
B I'm impressed! 我很佩服！

---

A My hard work finally bore fruit. 我的努力终于有了结果。
B I'm so proud of you. 我真以你为傲。

---

A I've been taking self-defense classes recently.
我最近在上防身术课程。 → self-defense 表示"自我防卫"
B Wow! You're really something. 哇！你真了不起。

**Part 3 美国人聊天都说这些话**

**相关会话群组记忆** 表达"失败、不成功、表现不好"

★ **It's no good.** ……………………………………………… 这不好。
★ **I'm not good at math.** …………………………… 我数学不好。
★ **I didn't do well on my exam.** ……… 我考试没考好。
★ **I didn't pass my driving test.** …… 我驾驶测验没通过。
★ **He lost this game.** ………………………………… 他输了这场比赛。
★ **Our plan failed.** ……………………………………… 我们的计划失败了。
★ **I failed in my English test.** ………… 我英语测验不及格。
★ **I failed to complete my job.** ……… 我没有完成我的工作。
★ **Her acting career is a failure.**
………………………………………………………………………… 她的表演生涯并不成功。
★ **My attempt ended in failure.** ……… 我的尝试失败了。

★ I didn't make it. ……………………………………………… 我没有成功。
★ My expectations turned out badly.
………………………………………………………………………… 我的期待结果很糟糕。
★ These problems defeated me. ………… 这些问题难倒我了。
  ↳ defeat 表示"击败"
★ That movie is a fiasco. ………………………… 那部电影是个大失败。
★ This concert is a flop. …………………………… 这场演唱会是个大失败。
★ This fashion show is a disaster.
  ↳ disaster 表示"彻底的失败" …………………… 这场时装秀是场大灾难。
★ Everything went wrong. ………………………… 每件事都错了。
★ The plan collapsed because of lack of finance.
………………………………………………………………………… 计划由于缺乏资金而失败。
★ It's a fool's errand. ………………………………… 这是徒劳无功。

★ My endeavors ended in disappointment.
　endeavour 表示"努力、尝试" ……………… 我的努力以失望告终。
★ She is just an also-ran. ……………………… 她只是个失败者。

★ You're on the wrong track. ……………………………… 你做错了。
　on the wrong track 表示"做错了或想法是错的"
★ All my efforts came to nothing. ………………… 我所有努力都白费了。
★ The project came to grief. ………………………… 项目最终失败了。
★ Everything was fouled up. ……………………… 所有事情都被搞砸了。
　foul up 表示"弄糟"
★ The outcome fell short of the standards. ………… 结果没有达到标准。
★ My travel plan fell through. ……………………… 我的旅游计划泡汤了。
　fall through 表示"未能实现、未能落实"
★ The performance fell flat. …………………………… 表演完全失败。
★ I tried to convince him but in vain. ………… 我试图说服他但是没用。
★ Our team went down 3-0 to the defending champion.
　go down 表示"被打败" ………… 我们的队伍以零比三输给上届冠军。
★ All my work came to naught. ………………… 我所有成果都化为乌有。
★ Her music career has been going downhill. … 她的音乐事业在走下坡路。
★ He made a dog's breakfast of the job. ……… 他把工作做得乱七八糟。
　a dog's breakfast 表示"把一件事做得乱七八糟"
★ I brought my eggs to a bad market. ……………………… 我失算了。
★ His business plan went up in smoke. ……… 他的事业计划以失败告终。
★ He hit the skids after he was fired. … 他被开除之后，生活开始走下坡路。
　hit the skids / be on the skids 表示"走下坡"
★ The proposal fizzled out. ………………………… 此计划逐渐终止。
★ She worked hard but missed the mark.
………………………………………… 她很努力，但还是没达到目标。
★ Violence leads to a dead end. ………………… 暴力到最后是死路一条。
★ A false step could lead to failure. ………………… 失策可能导致失败。
★ Now we're back to square one. ……………… 现在我们要从头开始了。
★ This just blew up in my face. ……………… 这件事情完全搞砸了。

### 听美国人聊天

**A** I lost this game. 我输了这场比赛。
**B** Well, don't give up. Keep going. 嗯,别放弃,继续坚持。

---

**A** How was your driving test? 你的驾驶测验考得如何?
**B** I didn't pass my driving test. 我驾驶测验没通过。

---

**A** Our plan came to nothing. 我们的计划都白费了。
**B** Now we're back to square one. 现在我们要从头开始了。

---

**A** Why do you look so worried? 你今天看起来怎么这么忧虑?
**B** I didn't do well on my English exam. 我英语考试没考好。

---

**A** Did you enjoy the party last night? 你享受昨晚的派对吗?
**B** No. The party was a washout. 不。派对很失败。

---

**A** Do you like this show? 你喜欢这场表演吗?
**B** No. The performance fell flat. 不喜欢。表演完全失败。

---

**A** Everything was fouled up. 所有事情都被搞砸了。
**B** Cheer up! Everything will be fine. 振作一点!一切都会没事的。

---

**A** I worked so hard but still missed the mark.
我很努力,却还是没达到目标。
**B** Keep it up. You will make progress. 继续努力,你会进步的。

---

**A** How's your research paper coming along?
你的研究报告有何进展?
**B** I'm totally on the wrong track. 我的方向完全错误。

---

**A** That film is a flop. 那部电影很失败。
**B** But I kind of like it. 但是我有点儿喜欢。

(美国人还会这样说) **其他与表达"非常成功"相关的惯用语**

## 1. have the world at your feet 前途无量

这个短语字面意思是"世界在你脚下",形容"很成功""前途无量""前程似锦"。

- This young man has the world at his feet.
  这个年轻人前途无量。

## 2. a feather in one's cap 令人值得骄傲的成就

feather 意思是"羽毛",cap 意思是"帽子",字面意思是"插在帽子上的羽毛",比喻"令人值得骄傲的成就"。

- This job is a feather in his cap.
  这份工作是他值得骄傲的成就。

## 3. the sky's the limit 无限可能

这个短语字面意思是"天空才是极限",比喻"可达到的成就没有极限"。

- I know I can make it. The sky's the limit.
  我知道我做得到,我拥有无限可能。

# Lesson 29  Once in a Blue Moon

## 难得一见

🗨 中文"难得一见",英语要如何表达呢?

就是"once in a blue moon"。blue moon 是"蓝月"的意思。蓝月是一种罕见的现象,月面呈现蓝色,因此这个短语是用来形容"难得一见""绝无仅有""千载难逢""不常发生"的事情。

- I drink coffee once in a blue moon.
  我很少喝咖啡。

- Once in a blue moon I make a mistake.
  我很少会犯错。

- You come to visit me once in a blue moon.
  你难得来拜访我。

- He only smokes once in a blue moon.
  他几乎不抽烟。

- They have a quarrel once in a blue moon.
  他们很少起争执。
  ↳ quarrel 表示"争执"

- Something like this happens once in a blue moon.
  像这样的事极少会发生。

(相关会话群组记忆) 表达事情"稀少、不寻常的、不常发生、难得一见、千载难逢"

★ **No way!** 较口语 …………………… 绝不！/ 当然不！
★ **Not likely!** 较口语 …………………… 绝对不可能！
★ **Not much.** 较口语 …………………… 不多。/ 很少。
★ **Not a bit.** …………………………………… 一点也不。
★ **It's unusual.** ……………………………… 这很不寻常。
★ **This is so special.** ……………………… 这很特别。
★ **It's very uncommon.** …………………… 这很不常见。
★ **It is somewhat interesting.** ………… 这有点儿趣味。
   somewhat 表示"有点儿、稍微"

★ **This is an exceptional experience.**
   ………………………………………………… 这是一个特殊的经验。

★ **This kind of accident is infrequent.**
   infrequent 表示"罕见的"…………………… 这种意外很少见。

★ **It's abnormal.** …………………………… 这不正常。
★ **This is a unique necklace.**
   ………………………………………………… 这是一条独一无二的项链。

★ **This is an atypical horror film.**
   ………………………………………………… 这是一部非典型的恐怖片。

★ **I hardly know you.** …………………… 我几乎不认识你。
★ **I hardly ever use Facebook.** ……… 我几乎不用脸书。
★ **Every so often I get up late.** ……… 我偶尔会晚起床。
   every so often 表示"偶尔、有时"

★ **There is hardly any space in this room.**
   ………………………………………… 这个房间几乎已经没有任何空间了。

★ **This is very rare.** ……………………… 这很少见。

★ **This is of rare occurrence.** 这很少发生。
★ **I rarely get sick.** 我很少生病。
★ **She seldom laughs.** 她很少笑。

seldom 当副词表示"很少、难得"

★ **It doesn't happen often.** 这不常发生。
★ **I like to dine out, but not very often.** 我喜欢外出用餐,但不经常去。

dine 表示"吃饭";dine out 表示"在外用餐"

★ **I scarcely talk to my mother.** 我很少跟我母亲谈话。
★ **She scarcely ever eats meat.** 她几乎从不吃肉。
★ **In South Africa, water is scarce.** 在南非,水很缺乏。
★ **He seldom or never drives his car.**

seldom or never 表示"极少、简直不" 他极少开他的车。

★ **He can barely walk after breaking his leg.** 他摔断腿后几乎没办法走路。
★ **I tell a lie occasionally.** 我偶尔会说谎。
★ **Trees are very sparse around this area.**

sparse 表示"数量稀少的" 这区域周围树非常稀少。

★ **I sporadically cook.** 我偶尔下厨。
★ **It is well-nigh impossible to live here.**

well-nigh 表示"几乎" 几乎不可能住在这里。

★ I almost never cry. 我几乎不哭。
★ I almost didn't pass the test. 我差点没通过测验。
★ I only just made it to work on time. 我差点没能准时上班。
★ You don't see this every day. 这不是每天都会发生的。

★ I met him a few times. ……………………… 我遇到过他几次。
　→ a few 表示"为数不多的、几个"
★ It happens in a few cases.
　………………………………… 在个别情况下，会发生这样的事。
★ He is not at all angry at me. …… 他一点儿也没有生我的气。
　↳ not at all 表示"一点儿都不"
★ It's not quite normal. ……………………………… 这不太正常。
★ On rare occasions I ride a bike to work.
　……………………………………………… 我偶尔会骑自行车去上班。
★ I work overtime on occasion. ………………… 我有时会加班。
★ He is by no means a decent man.
　↳ by no means 表示"绝不、一点儿也不"… 他绝不是一个正派的人。

★ We meet each other (every) now and then. ……… 我们偶尔才见面。
　↳ (every) now and then 表示"有时、偶尔"
★ I go to a movie once in a while. ……………………… 我偶尔会去看电影。
★ I drink wine once in a way. ………………………… 我偶尔会喝葡萄酒。
　↳ once in a way 表示"偶尔、只有一次、破例地"
★ At times I go fishing. ………………………………… 我有时会去钓鱼。
　↳ at times 表示"有时、偶尔"
★ I only wear a skirt once or twice a month.
　↳ once or twice 表示"一两次、几次"……… 我一个月只穿一两次裙子。
★ I read this book by fits and starts. …………… 我断断续续地看这本书。
★ I have been teaching English on and off for five years.
　↳ on and off 表示"断断续续地"………… 我断断续续教英语有五年了。
★ A decent man like him is few and far between.
　………………………………………………… 像他这样正直的人不多见。
★ This case is out of the ordinary. ……………… 这个例子非比寻常。
　↳ out of the ordinary 表示"非比寻常的、例外的、非凡的"
★ A chance like this is one in a million. …… 像这样的机会是极其少有的。
★ Great movies are thin on the ground. ………… 很棒的电影寥寥无几。

**听美国人聊天**

**A** What do you like to do in your free time?
你空闲时都做些什么?

**B** At times I go fishing. 我有时会去钓鱼。

---

**A** This is a unique necklace. It cost me a lot.
这是一条独一无二的项链。我花了很多钱。

**B** It's beautiful and so special. 这很漂亮而且非常特别。

---

**A** I heard you quit drinking. 我听说你戒酒了。

**B** I only drink once or twice a month. 我一个月只喝一两次(酒)。

---

**A** I saw a rat chasing a cat today. 今天我看到一只老鼠在追一只猫。

**B** You don't see this every day. 这不是每天都会发生的。

---

**A** I haven't seen Eric lately. How has he been?
很久没看到埃里克了,他过得如何?

**B** He's been sick. He can barely walk after breaking his leg. 他生病了。他摔断腿后几乎没办法走路。

---

**A** Do you like to travel? 你喜欢旅游吗?

**B** Yes, I like to travel, but not very often.
是,我喜欢旅游,但不经常旅游。

---

**A** Can I add you on Facebook? 我可以在脸书加你为好友吗?

**B** I hardly ever use it. 我几乎没在用。

---

**A** I can't believe it snows here in September.
真不敢相信这里竟然在九月下雪。

**B** It's very unusual. 这很不寻常。

**相关会话群组记忆** 表达"很常见、很有规律、频率很高"

- ★ **I eat a lot.** 我吃得很多。
- ★ **It's very common.** 这很常见。
- ★ **I usually take a walk after dinner.**
  我经常晚餐后散步。
- ★ **My family often go camping.**
  我的家人常常去露营。
- ★ **He starts to smoke frequently.**
  他开始频繁地抽烟。
- ★ **The meeting is held regularly.** 会议定期举办。
- ★ **I generally take the subway to school.**
  我一般都坐地铁去上学。
- ★ **I told you repeatedly not to be late for class.**
  我再三告诉过你上课不要迟到。
- ★ **Most people just constantly complain about everything.** 大部分的人只是不停地抱怨所有事情。
- ★ **I periodically see a psychiatrist.**
  我定期去看心理医生。
- ★ **Customarily, pregnant women can't dye their hair.** 习俗上,孕妇不能染发。

- ★ I do all the housework as usual.
  一如往常,我做所有的家事。
- ★ I make it a rule to read every day.
  ↪ make it a rule 表示"定为常规" 我把阅读定为每天的常规。

★ She just complains all the time. ……………… 她一直在抱怨。
　↳ all the time 表示"一直、无时无刻"
★ I met her many a time. …………………… 我遇到过她很多次。
★ Don't do this over and over again.
　…………………………………… 不要一而再，再而三地这么做。
★ The same thing happens time after time.
　↳ time after time 表示"一再、屡次"………… 相同的事情一再发生。
★ In many instances this doesn't work.
　………………………………………… 在很多情况下这没有用。
★ You did the right thing on the whole.
　…………………………………………… 大体上你做了正确的事。

---

★ My life is as regular as clockwork. ……………… 我的生活很有规律。
　↳ as regular as clockwork 表示"很有规律"
★ It rains in the afternoon here as often as not.
　↳ as often as not 表示"往往、多半"………… 这里往往下午会下雨。
★ More often than not I have a cup of black tea in the morning.
　………………………………………… 我通常早上会喝杯红茶。
★ Cleaning is all in a day's work for me. ………… 打扫是我的日常工作。
　↳ all in a day's work 表示"每日生活中的一部分"
★ As a rule, I jog every morning. ……………… 通常我每天早上都会慢跑。
　↳ as a rule 表示"通常、照例"
★ This is just a run-of-the-mill movie. ………… 这只是一部普通的电影。
★ This ring is a dime a dozen. ↗较口语 ……………… 这个戒指很普通。
★ I check my email every day as a matter of course.
　…………………………………………… 我照例每天查看我的电子邮件。
　↳ as a matter of course 表示"照例、理所当然"
★ Nine times out of ten he is late for work. ……… 他十有八九会迟到。
　↳ nine times out of ten 表示"十有八九、几乎总是"
★ It's par for the course. ……………………………… 这是意料中的事。
　↳ par for the course 表示"司空见惯、常有的事、意料中的事"

**听美国人聊天**

- A: I met Daisy many a time. She just complained all the time.
  我遇到黛西很多次,她总是不停地在抱怨。
- B: That's annoying. 那很讨厌。

---

- A: Your house is so clean. 你的房子好干净。
- B: Thank you. Cleaning is all in a day's work for me.
  谢谢。打扫是我的日常工作。

---

- A: I've tried pig's blood cake. It's yummy!
  我尝试了猪血糕,真好吃!
- B: It's a very common snack in Taiwan. 这是台湾很常见的点心。

---

- A: What do you do on weekends? 你周末都做些什么?
- B: I usually go shopping. 我通常去逛街。

---

- A: Nine times out of ten he is late for work.
  他上班十有八九会迟到。
- B: Old habits die hard! 老习惯很难改!

---

- A: You look well. How do you keep fit?
  你气色很好,你是如何保持健康的?
- B: I make it a rule to exercise every day. 每天运动是我的惯例。

---

- A: What's your favorite food? 你最喜欢的食物是什么?
- B: Spaghetti. I eat spaghetti many times a week.
  意大利面。我一个星期吃好几次。

---

- A: Hey, check out my new necklace! 嘿,看一下我的新项链!
- B: It's a dime a dozen. Nothing special.
  这很普通。没什么特别的。

Part 3 美国人聊天都说这些话

(美国人还会这样说) **其他与表达"难得一见"相关的惯用语**

### 1. once-in-a-lifetime 很难得

这个短语字面上的意思是"一生只有一次",形容事物"很难得"。

- Studying abroad is a once-in-a-lifetime chance.
  出国留学是一生难得的机会。

### 2. when pigs fly 绝不可能

这个短语字面上的意思是"当猪会飞的时候",表示"绝不可能"。

- She will get married when pigs fly.
  她绝不可能结婚。

### 3. as scarce as hen's teeth 非常罕见

hen 意思是"母鸡",这个短语字面上的意思是"如同母鸡的牙齿一样罕见",形容事物"十分罕见""极其稀有"。

- A job like this is as scarce as hen's teeth.
  像这样的工作非常罕见。

# Lesson 30  Great Minds Think Alike

## 我也这么觉得

Part 3 美国人聊天都说这些话

● 中文"英雄所见略同"翻成英语要怎么说呢？

就是"Great minds think alike"。great 表示"伟大的"，mind 表示"头脑、心智"，think 就是"思考"，alike 则是"相同的"，所以整句话的意思就是，很聪明的人都有一样的想法。美国人说这句话时，通常表示"双方很有默契，想法不谋而合"。

- Great minds think alike. I also think that people should respect each other.
  英雄所见略同，我也认为人们应该彼此尊重。

- We came up with the same idea. Great minds think alike.
  我们提出了相同的点子。英雄所见略同啊！

- Great minds think alike, so I followed your advice.
  英雄所见略同，所以我听从你的建议。

- Great minds think alike, so I agree with you.
  英雄所见略同，所以我同意你的看法。

- We are on the same page. Great minds think alike.
  我们意见一致，真是英雄所见略同。
  ↳ on the same page 表示"意见一致"

- Great minds think alike, so we all love this movie.
  英雄所见略同，所以我们都爱这部电影。

239

(相关会话群组记忆) 表达"同意、认同、附议"

★ **Absolutely! / Exactly!** 较口语 ……… 当然！/ 没错！
★ **Count me in.** 较口语 …………………… 算我一份。
★ **Ditto.** 较口语 ……………………………… 我也一样。
★ **Fair enough.** ……………………………… 有道理。
★ **Fine. / Good.** ……………………………… 很好。
★ **Good idea.** ………………………………… 好主意。
★ **I agree.** 任何情况皆适用 …………………… 我赞同。
★ **I guess so.** ………………………………… 我想也是。
★ **I'll say!** …………………………………… 可不是嘛！
★ **I'm for it.** …………………………………… 我赞成。
★ **I second that.** ……………………………… 我附议。
★ **I totally agree.** ……………………………… 我完全同意。
★ **That's right.** ………………………………… 没错。
★ **That's true.** ………………………………… 没错。
★ **Of course.** ………………………………… 当然。
★ **You bet!** 较口语 …………………………… 当然！/ 没错！
★ **You are correct.** …………………………… 你是正确的。
★ **You are right.** ……………………………… 你是对的。
★ **I feel the same way.** ……………………… 我有同感。

★ I couldn't agree more. ……………… 我完全同意你的看法。
★ I have no objections. ……………………… 我没有异议。
　　objection 表示"反对"，也可表示"disapproval（不赞同）"
★ I'm down with that. 较口语 ……………………… 我同意。

- ★ I'm fine with that. 我没异议。/ 没问题。
- ★ I'm completely with you. 我完全支持你。
- ★ I'm OK with that decision. 那个决定我没问题。
- ★ That makes sense. 那说得通。
- ★ That sounds like a great idea. 那听起来是个好主意。
- ★ We agree with what you said. 我们赞同你所说的。
- ★ We approve what you said. 我们赞同你所说的。
- ★ We are on the same page. ☞较口语 我们意见一致。

(30-04)

- ★ Everything you said is true. 你说的每件事都是真的。
- ★ I'm on board. / I'm on board with that. 我加入。/ 我同意。
- ★ I'm on your side when it comes to this matter. ☞较正式
  涉及这件事情时,我是支持你的。
- ★ I'm siding with Jack on this argument.
  这场争论我是站在杰克这一边的。
  ☞ argument 表示"较为激烈的争论",相较之下 discussion 是"较为温和的讨论"
- ★ No, I don't think you were wrong. 不,我觉得你没错。
- ★ Now you're talking! 这才像话!
- ★ Tell me about it! ☞表示附和(较口语) 可不是吗?/ 就是说嘛!
- ★ That's a good point. 那是个好观点。
  ☞ 常用于会议中。也可以把 point 换成 idea、suggestion、proposal
- ★ That makes two of us. 我跟你有同感。
- ★ That is exactly what I was thinking. 那跟我想得一模一样。
- ★ You are absolutely correct on this matter.
  在这件事情上你绝对是正确的。
- ★ You can say that again. 你说得没错。
- ★ You made the right decision. 你做了个正确的决定。
  ☞ make... decision 表示"做……决定"

Part 3 美国人聊天都说这些话

## 听美国人聊天

**A** This winter is not cold at all. 今年冬天一点儿也不冷。
**B** That's true. 没错。

---

**A** The party was a lot of fun. 派对很好玩。
**B** Absolutely! I enjoyed it a lot. 当然！我玩得很开心。

---

**A** This is a tough decision to make. 这是个困难的决定。
　　→ tough 表示"费力的"
**B** I agree. 我赞同。

---

**A** We should adopt his proposal. 我们应该采用他的提议。
**B** I'm for it. 我赞成。

---

**A** Kevin is such a nice guy. 凯文真是个好人。
**B** That's right. I like him, too. 没错。我也喜欢他。

---

**A** How about trying that new restaurant tonight?
今晚去吃那家新餐厅如何？
**B** That sounds like a great idea. 那听起来是个好主意。

---

**A** This class is so boring, isn't it? 这堂课好无聊，是不是？
**B** I couldn't agree more. 我完全同意你的看法。

---

**A** I can't believe it's so hot in March and April.
我不敢相信三四月这么热。
**B** Tell me about it! 可不是嘛！

---

**A** The housing price in Taipei is Beijing high.
台北的房价像北京那么高。
**B** I totally agree. 我完全同意。

**相关会话群组记忆** 表达"反对、不相信、感到怀疑"

★ **Absolutely not!** ……………………………… 当然不!
★ **Are you serious?** …………………………… 你是认真的吗?
★ **Far from it.** 较口语 ………… 根本不是。/ 一点儿也不。
★ **I beg to differ. / I beg to disagree.** 较礼貌的说法
………………………………………………… 恕我无法同意。

beg 表示"请求、允许"; differ 表示"意见不同"

★ **I don't agree.** 任何情况皆适用 …………………… 我不认同。
★ **I don't agree with you.** …………… 我不同意你的看法。
★ **I don't agree with you on this point.**
………………………………………… 我不同意你的这一点。
★ **I don't buy it!** ………………………………… 我不相信!

buy 表示"相信、同意"

★ **I don't think so.** …………………………… 我不这么认为。
★ **I doubt it.** ……………………………………… 我很怀疑。

★ **I doubt whether it's true or not.** …… 我怀疑这是不是真的。
★ **I'm afraid I don't agree with you.** … 我恐怕不同意你的看法。
★ **I'm completely against it.** ………………… 我完全反对这件事。

against 表示"反对"

★ **I'm sorry but I don't agree with you on this.**
………………………………………… 很抱歉,我不同意你这一点。
★ **I object!** ………………………………………… 我反对!
★ **I smell a rat.** ……………………………… 我觉得很可疑。

smell a rat 是俚语。字面上的意思是"闻到一只老鼠",表示"觉得某事很可疑"

★ I strongly disagree with you. ……… 我坚决不同意你的看法。
★ I totally disagree. …………………………………… 我完全不同意。
★ It doesn't make sense. ……………………………… 这不合理。

---

★ It sounds fishy. ……………………………………………… 听起来很可疑。
  ↳ fishy 除了"鱼腥味"的意思,也表示"可疑的"。
★ It's not like that. ……………………………………………… 并不是这样。
★ No way. ↳较口语 ……………………………………………………… 绝不。
★ Nonsense! ……………………………………………………… 胡说!
★ Of course not! ………………………………………………… 当然不!
★ On the contrary. ……………………………………………… 正好相反。
★ That doesn't make sense. …………………………………… 那没道理。
★ That doesn't sound right. …………………………………… 听起来不对。
★ This is all wrong. …………………………………………… 这大错特错。
★ That's a bad idea. …………………………………………… 那是个馊主意。
★ That's impossible. …………………………………………… 那不可能。
★ That's not a good idea. ……………………………………… 那不是个好主意。
★ That's not true. ……………………………………………… 那不是真的。
★ That's out of the question. …………………………………… 那不可能。
  ↳ out of the question 表示"不可能的"
★ You are totally wrong. ……………………………………… 你大错特错。

---

**关键单词短语**

| against | differ | disagree |
|---|---|---|
| ⓟ 反对 | ⓥ 意见不同 | ⓥ 不同意 |
| **fishy** | **object** | |
| ⓐ 可疑的 | ⓥ 反对 | |

- **smell a rat** 觉得可疑
- **out of the question** 不可能

**听美国人聊天**

A　Do you want to go shopping with me this Saturday?
你这星期六想跟我去逛街吗?

B　That's not a good idea. 那不是个好主意。

---

A　Allen is very stingy and selfish. 艾伦非常小气且自私。

B　I don't agree. 我不认同。　→ stingy 表示"小气的"

---

A　Can we have a second honeymoon? 我们能不能有第二次蜜月?

B　That's out of the question. It costs a lot of money.
不可能,那要花很多钱。

---

A　We can do without a cell phone. 我们没有手机也行。
→ do without 表示"没有……也行"

B　I'm afraid I don't agree with you. 我恐怕不能同意你的看法。

---

A　I'm going to go on a diet from today. 从今天起我要开始节食。

B　Are you serious? 你是认真的吗?

---

A　This plan was a total fiasco. 这次计划彻底失败了。

B　You are totally wrong. 你大错特错。

---

A　Married women shouldn't work. 已婚的女人不应该工作。

B　I'm sorry but I don't agree with you on this.
很抱歉,我不同意你这一观点。

---

A　Do you believe in ghosts? 你相信有鬼吗?

B　Of course not! 当然不!

---

A　You don't care about me at all. 你根本不在乎我。

B　That's not true. 那不是真的。

## 美国人还会这样说  其他与表达"意见"相关的惯用语

### 1. beat around the bush  拐弯抹角、绕圈子

beat 是"打、拍",bush 是"矮树丛",around the bush 是"绕着矮树丛"。全句字面上的意思是"绕着矮树丛拍打",引申为说话不直接、即"绕圈子""拐弯抹角"。

- Don't beat around the bush. You're wasting my time.
  说话别拐弯抹角。你在浪费我的时间。

### 2. cut to the chase  直接切入主题

cut 是"切",chase 是"追逐",cut to the chase 意思是"直接切入主题""开门见山"。

- Let's cut to the chase. Do you want to marry me?
  我们直接切入主题吧,你要不要跟我结婚?

### 3. get the picture  理解、了解情况

get 是"了解",picture 除了"图片",还有"局面"的意思。get the picture 是"了解情况""理解"的意思。

- Now I get the picture. You've been lying to me.
  现在我了解了,你一直对我说谎。

版权专有　侵权必究

## 图书在版编目（CIP）数据

英语的逻辑：30天学会美国人的英语逻辑 / 刘婉瑀著. —北京：北京理工大学出版社，2019.7
ISBN 978-7-5682-7230-8

Ⅰ.①英⋯　Ⅱ.①刘⋯　Ⅲ.①英语—自学参考资料　Ⅳ.①H31

中国版本图书馆CIP数据核字（2019）第135032号

北京市版权局著作权合同登记号图字：01-2017-2395
简体中文版由我识出版社有限公司授权出版发行
英文的逻辑：用老外的逻辑思考，才能真正学好英文，刘婉瑀
著，2015年，初版
ISBN：9789864070145

| | | | |
|---|---|---|---|
| 出版发行 / | 北京理工大学出版社有限责任公司 | | |
| 社　　址 / | 北京市海淀区中关村南大街5号 | | |
| 邮　　编 / | 100081 | | |
| 电　　话 / | （010）68914775（总编室） | | |
| | （010）82562903（教材售后服务热线） | | |
| | （010）68948351（其他图书服务热线） | | |
| 网　　址 / | http://www.bitpress.com.cn | | |
| 经　　销 / | 全国各地新华书店 | | |
| 印　　刷 / | 河北鸿祥信彩印刷有限公司 | | |
| 开　　本 / | 787毫米×1092毫米　1/32 | | |
| 印　　张 / | 8 | 责任编辑 / | 潘　昊 |
| 字　　数 / | 246千字 | 文案编辑 / | 潘　昊 |
| 版　　次 / | 2019年7月第1版　2019年7月第1次印刷 | 责任校对 / | 周瑞红 |
| 定　　价 / | 32.00元 | 责任印制 / | 李志强 |

图书出现印装质量问题，请拨打售后服务热线，本社负责调换